The Economy of Tanganyika

TANGANYIKA

KEY
——— Main Roads
+–+–+ Railways
———— International Boundaries
·········· District Boundaries
──────── Provincial Boundaries

0   Miles   100   200

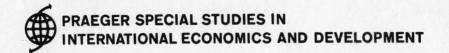

PRAEGER SPECIAL STUDIES IN
INTERNATIONAL ECONOMICS AND DEVELOPMENT

The Economy of Tanganyika

Gilbert L. Rutman

FREDERICK A. PRAEGER, Publishers
New York · Washington · London

The purpose of the Praeger Special Studies is to make specialized research monographs in U.S. and international economics and politics available to the academic, business, and government communities. For further information, write to the Special Projects Division, Frederick A. Praeger, Publishers, 111 Fourth Avenue, New York, N.Y. 10003.

FREDERICK A. PRAEGER, PUBLISHERS
111 Fourth Avenue, New York, N.Y. 10003, U.S.A.
77-79 Charlotte Street, London W.1, England

Published in the United States of America in 1968
by Frederick A. Praeger, Inc., Publishers

Library of Congress Catalog Card Number: 67-25247

Printed in the United States of America

In Memory of My Father

ABRAHAM E. RUTMAN

PREFACE

On April 22, 1964, Tanganyika merged with Zanzibar to form a new political state, which was named Tanzania on April 29, 1964. The scope of this study is restricted, however, to an investigation of Tanganyika's economic system; and I shall refer herein to this part of Tanzania by its former name.

This study is an attempt to analyze the efforts of Tanganyika's new political leaders to stimulate economic growth, to build a socialistic economy, and to create a unified political state. In the spring of 1964, Julius Nyerere, President of Tanganyika, announced to Parliament that a new experiment in the area of economic planning was to be tried, beginning in that year. This study is concerned with the conditions existing at the time that this new form of planning was implemented, the nature of the plans, and the probable effects. While no attempt is made to examine the effects of each provision of this plan, an evaluation is made as to the likelihood that the over-all aims will be achieved.

The approach used is to emphasize the weaknesses of Tanganyika's economic system in order to shed additional light on the forces impeding economic growth. By such an approach, it is hoped that remedies will be more easily found. There is no attempt to blame a particular person or group of people for failing to achieve a given goal; quite the contrary, I admire the sincerity and unselfishness with which the leaders devote themselves to achieving a higher standard of living for the people. I personally feel that the problem lies in the magnitude of the changes needed, not in the lack of qualified or competent African leaders.

The idea for making such a study emanated from discussions and seminars with Calvin B. Hoover, whose life work has been dedicated to an examination of the role of government in the economic process. In preparing this study, I have greatly benefited from his advice and assistance as well as that of Joseph J. Spengler. I wish to thank the Ford Foundation for making available financial assistance so that I could visit Tanganyika, the National Science Foundation for providing a grant so that I could update the data, and the Division of Economic Research of the University of Arizona for providing released teaching time. I wish also to thank the many people in Tanganyika who aided in the collection of data, and most especially, Miss C. Peters and Mrs. D. Calvin of the Boston University African Library for their many hours spent in searching for information. In the area of organizing and typing this material, there are a whole host of people to whom I wish to express my appreciation; a few of these are my wife, Roanne, Mrs. C. Rehfield, Mr. J. DeSando, and Mrs. Joyce Drennen. Needless to say, the opinions expressed herein are strictly my own.

Gilbert Rutman

CONTENTS

LIST OF TABLES

LIST OF FIGURES

The Economy of Tanganyika

INTRODUCTION

On December 9, 1961, Tanganyika achieved its independence after seventy-seven years of European rule.[1] Of
these seventy-seven years, thirty-three were spent under
German domination and forty-four under British administration. Britain ruled Tanganyika, first, as a mandate under
the League of Nations and, later, as a trusteeship under the
United Nations.[2]

Before departing, the British attempted to establish a
multiparty democratic form of government. The existence of
two parties, however, never became a reality. The Tanganyika National Union (TANU) captured all of the parliamentary
seats in the first general election of 1958-59;[3] and since 1959,
for all practical purposes, only one party has existed.[4]

Julius Nyerere, President of Tanganyika,[5] maintains
that his nation is a democracy, even though it is a one-party
state. He claims that the presence of a loyal opposition party
is not a prerequisite to a democracy, if the existence of one
party is the result of the people's free expression at the polls.
Secondly, freedom of choice in the selection of candidates
has been maintained by allowing more than one candidate to
seek the privilege of being the TANU nominee.[6] In addition,
Nyerere believes that a two-party state is necessary to preserve democracy only in Western countries where there is
competition between socio-economic classes over the ownership of the means of production and the consequent distribution of income. In Tanganyika, a two-party system is unnecessary, because the society is basically classless. This is
due to the majority of the people living under traditional
principles of tribalism, which are essentially egalitarian in
nature.[7] Further, because of the people's belief that TANU
is the protector and the promoter of the best interests of the
nation as a whole, it is felt that any challenge is regarded by
the people as traitorous and thus presents a threat to the
political peace and stability of the country.[8]

On July 7, 1962, Nyerere began his political maneuver-
ing to make Tanganyika into a one-party state. On this date,
Nyerere warned all opposition parties to "behave or be
banned."[9] Mr. Zubert Mtemvu, President of the African

National Congress Party, defended the right of opposition
parties to criticize the government in power by retorting,
"It was creditable to abuse the government in colonial days.
But this cannot be so today, because there is a people's
government."[10] In January, 1963, Nyerere moved to gain
statutory recognition for a one-party system. He stated,
"Inasmuch as people only recognize one party, the laws of
the country must also recognize only one party."[11] In order
to insure that Tanganyika remained a "democratic" one-party
state, Nyerere stated that the electoral procedure would be
revised so that more than one candidate could seek TANU
endorsement. The contests would be run on an individual
rather than party basis, i.e., the individual selected would
have to receive the support of TANU's rank-and-file members.[12]

    Nyerere, however, declared that all of TANU's Mem-
bers of Parliament would have to be approved by the party's
officers and be required to maintain discipline in Parliament
by adhering to the principles and policies set by the party.[13]
In the early part of 1963, the opposition party, the Tanganyika National Congress, had its registration cancelled by the
Ministry of Home Affairs. The official reason given was,
"The party was being used for unlawful purposes prejudicial
to or incompatible with the maintenance of good order and
good government."[14] In January, 1964, Nyerere appointed a
thirteen-man commission to consider constitutional changes
necessary to put into effect a democratic one-party state.[15]
The Commission reported to the president in 1965 on the procedural changes.[16] In March, 1964, Sheikh Armi Abede,
Minister for Justice, summarized the government's position
toward Western-style democracy: "Opposition parties in
African states had proved to be a failure and had brought con-
fusion to the people. Africa had its own traditional type of
democracy which must be recovered immediately to blot out
the wrong and bookish foreign democracy."[17]

    The government has also tightened its control over the
activities of pressure groups within the country in order to
maintain peace and stability. On March 23, 1962, approximately four months after independence, Mr. Nsilo Swai, then
Minister for Commerce and Industry, warned that any newspaper which published inflamatory matter, which was considered liable to undermine the unity of the people or provoke

unrest in the country, would be closed.[18] On June 28, 1962,
the General Assembly passed the Trade Disputes Settlement
Bill, which outlawed strikes.[19] On September 27, 1962, the
General Assembly passed the Detention Bill, authorizing the
government to detain indefinitely without a trial any person
considered a threat to the continued stability and security of
the state.[20] The Presidential Commission of 1965 opposed
the passage of a Bill of Rights on grounds that it could lead
to a conflict with the state's responsibility to protect the existing system against subversion.[21]

     The elimination of all opposition to the political leaders
has created a new class in Tanganyika, which, for all practical purposes, rules the nation.[22] Membership in the political
elites of the new African states has generally been based on
education and wealth.[23] In a survey of college graduates
from Makerere College (Kampala, Uganda), J. E. Goldthorpe
found that graduates came invariably from large landowner
families, and almost always sought government service as a
career.[24] The importance of education as a criterion for
elite status is emphasized by Edward Shils:

     It is not so much what education teaches, as it is
     the fact that the experience of having been to
     school, especially in countries with a steeply
     graded system of social stratification and a tra-
     dition of the superiority of the religiously educat-
     ed, gives to those who have been to school an
     enhanced feeling of their own value. It makes
     them feel that they have acquired some extremely
     valuable qualities which entitle them to the respect
     of others.[25]

     The major political goals of the elite group are the pro-
motion of national unity and African nationalism. Nyerere has
stressed that the first step in the process of unity is the elimination of tribal loyalties and rivalries[26] and the instillment
of national pride.[27] African nationalism amounts to the re-
placement of non-African influence with that of the new elite.
The fight of the leaders against non-African influence includes
that of groups within as well as outside of Tanganyika and is
aimed at redressing past inequities. As Fred Burke states,
"For East African groups, political independence alone cannot
restore a damaged ego or a loss of identity. The continued

presence of Europeans and Asians in positions of authority,
influence, and affluence is a constant reminder that the
African is still regarded with contempt. "[28]

Tanganyika's political leaders have two main economic
objectives: (1) to increase substantially the rate of economic
growth, and (2) to Africanize the economy. Africanization
refers to putting an African stamp on the economy by replac-
ing non-Africans in decision-making positions with Africans.
These two goals often conflict; in such cases, Africanization
has a higher priority.

The political leaders adopted an ideology, called African
Socialism, as a means of achieving these economic goals.
This ideology has not been clearly defined, and, thus, the
difference in meaning between it and that type of "socialism,"
which is discussed for possible adoption in Western nations,[29]
remains vague. [30]

John B. George described African Socialism, in a negative manner, as a concept ". . . which outlaws freehold land
tenure and brushes aside other motivations of property and
private enterprise. "[31] One of the major reasons "African
Socialism" remains vague is that Africa's political leaders
fear that their position of nonalignment in the cold war could
be lost if they openly adopted an ideology similar to that of the
Soviet Union. [32] Bethwell Ogot noted that many African
leaders were now claiming that it was unnecessary to define
it precisely, because all who believed in this ideology knew
its meaning intuitively. [33]

Generally, "African Socialism" refers to the organization of society along communal or collective lines. Julius
Nyerere conceived of a socialistic society springing up from
the communal relationship experienced in the extended family
of tribal society. [34] He believes sincerely that African Socialism will be a natural outgrowth from tribal society, where the
African feels that his interests are bound up with those of his
kinsmen. Initiative to speed up the process will be supplied
by the government.

There is a clear-cut distinction between the aims of
African Socialism and its Western counterpart. Western style
socialism is an attempt to eliminate the unequal distribution

of income in society, caused by the unequal distribution of the
means of production. African Socialism is not concerned with
this problem, as the following story illustrates. An African
official was asked by a British visitor if there was an essential difference between these two types of socialism. The
African replied that the Western version called for the government to seize all of the means of production in order to insure
an equitable distribution of income. In Tanganyika, the problem which confronts the leaders is not one of income distribution, but one of low national income. That is, the problem is
a shortage of the means of production to create income, rather
than who owns these means. African Socialism is, thus, a
method of accumulating capital, expanding the resource base,
and promoting African participation in commercial life. [35]

see p. 28

There are four reasons why socialism was chosen in
preference to free enterprise. First, there is a lack of
familiarity with the western concept of private property.
Most Africans still live within tribal jurisdiction, where the
right to earn income from assets without work, as well as the
right of free disposal of these assets through exchange, is
foreign. Secondly, there is a lack of a private African entrepreneurial class upon whom the responsibility for initiating
economic action could fall. The educated class is primarily
seeking governmental careers; and since 1962, the government
has been undergoing a process of Africanization. In 1962,
only 14 per cent of the civil service was composed of Africans.
By 1964, however, this figure had risen to forty-seven, and
by 1980, it is expected to rise to seventy-eight. [36]

At the present time, most commercial activities are
handled by the Asian segment of the population. These people
are viewed by most Africans as aliens who have used their
dominant position in commerce to exploit them. In the wake
of the mutiny of 1963, large mobs of Africans gathered in the
Asian quarters of Dar Es Salaam and paraded through the area
looting shops and shouting, "Colonialists Go Home!"[37]   Mr.
George Kahama, Minister for Commerce and Industry, asked
these Asian traders not to sabotage the African's efforts to
enter commercial activity. Kahama alleged that certain Asian
businessmen had created a "defense fund" to prevent the establishment of African retail cooperatives. Those traders
who lost money by undercutting the prices of these cooperatives were supposedly reimbursed from this fund. Kahama

warned the Asians that their trading privileges would be re-
voked unless they ceased such practices. [38]

From the leaders' treatment of the Asians, it appears
that African nationalism and African Socialism are two sides
of the same coin. "African nationalism" refers to the elimination of non-African political power, while "African Socialism" includes the elimination of non-African economic power.

Thirdly, the system of free enterprise has become
stereotyped as another form of colonialism. The political
leaders lean toward greater governmental control, because
they believe that a free enterprise system would eventually
lead to foreign domination. This is not to say that the leaders
are discouraging foreign private investment; in fact, they
have openly coveted it. [39] The leaders fear, however, that
foreign domination could occur if foreign investors were given
unrestricted rights to exploit their natural resources and
markets. Kamaliza stated that government policy called for
public ownership of at least 50 per cent of all large firms. [40]
This policy is not confined to investments by Western sources.
Nyerere has stated that a new form of imperialism has appeared in Africa. Socialist countries are now using wealth
for capitalistic purposes--to acquire power and prestige. [41]

And lastly, the major political goal--to create a unified
political state--is fostered by the government's position in
the economy. The political leaders have invested in enterprises which will build up a sense of national pride among
Tanganyika's various tribal groups. In effect, they have
established industries or financed projects to increase Tanganyika's prestige, even though the profitability of such investments is highly questionable.

The Study

The purpose of this study is to examine the government's
efforts to increase substantially Tanganyika's growth rate and
process of Africanizing the political-economic system. It is
suggested that: (1) a substantial increase in its growth rate is
doubtful, because of the nature of the existing economic system;
and (2) a substantial increase is made even more uncertain by
adding the second goal, because these two objectives often
conflict.

To state that Tanganyika's data are skimpy in coverage and inaccurate in content is to reiterate a characteristic of almost all African countries. [42] It should be noted, however, that the collection of national income data in these nations is relatively new; in many cases, the presentation of yearly estimates was started as late as the early 1950's. In addition, a large percentage of the estimates are based on subjective evaluations, especially with respect to subsistence production. This type of reporting is, of course, highly inaccurate, because the magnitudes change when the estimator changes. In many cases, the information is useless. For example, estimates of capital formation in the subsistence sector include solely activity in hut building. Regardless of these problems, the data available are useful in presenting an over-all picture of the nature of Tanganyika's economic system.

CHAPTER **1** NATURAL AND
POPULATION
RESOURCES

Tanganyika is located on the east coast of Africa, bor-
dered by three lakes--Victoria, Tanganyika, and Nyasa--and
the Indian Ocean. It is bounded on the north by Kenya and
Uganda; on the west by the Republic of the Congo, Ruanda,
and Urundi; and on the south by Portuguese Mozambique.[1]
Tanganyika's total area is 361,800 square miles, which includes 20,650 square miles of inland water and 4,350 square
miles of swamp area. It is almost the size of France,
Germany, and Belgium combined, or more than six times
the size of England.

The purpose of this chapter is to examine the size and
nature of Tanganyika's resource base in order to point out
its possible contribution to economic development. In so
doing, it will be indicated that Tanganyika does not possess
a large supply of economically exploitable natural resources,
nor is the present quality of its population conducive to a
rapid change in the economic structure. For discussion
purposes, this chapter is divided into two parts: (1) natural
resources and (2) population characteristics.

NATURAL RESOURCES

Land

Tanganyika's land area is classified by types of vegetation in Table 1. The classification "vegetation actively induced by man" is used as a measure of the agricultural land.
It includes: (1) land presently being cultivated, and (2) land
formerly cultivated and now abandoned. Category (2) refers
to the land which has been abandoned because of soil erosion.[2]
This measure of total agricultural land excludes, however,
land which could be cultivated with the aid of capital improvements such as drainage and clearance projects, irrigation
schemes, and pest control projects. For example, the

9

TABLE 1

TYPES OF VEGETATION
(as of December 31, 1959)[a]

Types of Vegetation	Total Area Covered (Square Miles)	Percentage of Total Area Covered
Closed Forest	4,270	1.3
Forest Woodland, Intermediate	1,680	.5
Woodland, Miombo	118,420	35.2
Woodland, Bushland Intermediate	14,740	4.4
Bushland and Thicket	40,050	11.9
Wooded Grassland	91,830	27.3
Grassland	33,870	10.1
Desert and Semi-Desert	2,030	.6
Vegetation Actively Induced by Man	29,900	8.9
Total Dry Land	336,800	100.0

[a]A different classification of.the dry land of Tanganyika is presented in Europa Yearbook: 1963.

Source: Tanganyika, Statistical Abstract: 1963, p. 3.

International Bank for Reconstruction and Development (IBRD)
mission states that around 4 million acres could be added by
irrigation or flood control;[3] this would increase the amount of
land in agricultural use by over 20 per cent.

There are no statistics available by which the size of
Tanganyika's pastoral land can be measured. The IBRD
mission and the East Africa Royal Commission classify as
pasture land all land which is not used in crop production
and receives only 20 inches or less of rain per year.[4] This
amounts to saying that all land not fit for crop production is
pastoral. The presence of the tsetse fly, however, over
more than half of Tanganyika's land surface and the season-
able rainfalls and floodings, which restrict the availability
of grass to certain times of the year, prevent such a classification from yielding accurate estimates. In general, the
land used as pastoral is of low quality. In fact, the land
which is used around Lake Victoria is reputed to be among
the worst in the world.[5]

Three major factors which impede the use of larger
tracts of Tanganyika for crop production are: (1) the presence of the tsetse fly, (2) the rocky nature of the terrain,
and (3) the lack of rainfall.[6] The problem of obtaining an
adequate supply of water is due not only to the small amount
of rainfall that falls annually in each region, but also to its
unreliability and high intensity. The only areas of Tanganyika with favorable rainfall conditions for the cultivation of
crops are those with a chance only of zero to five years out
of 100 of not receiving thirty inches per year.[7] Using such
a classification, Tanganyika has only four small arable
areas: (1) a small coastal area, (2) the lake shore, (3) most
of the Southern Highlands,[8] and (4) areas along the western
border. In summary, it is the peripheral areas which have
adequate rainfalls to warrant the economic production of
crops. The Lake Region is the most highly favored area
with respect to crop production.[9]

No general conclusions, however, can be made about
the relationship between the average annual rates of precip-
itation and the amount of dry land classified as agricultural.
While the Lake Region is Tanganyika's wettest area and has
the largest percentage of its dry land classified as agricultural (21.1 per cent), the Central Region is reputed to be the

driest[10] and yet has the next largest percentage of its dry
land classified as agricultural (14 per cent). The explanation is, as mentioned above, that much of Tanganyika is infested with the tsetse fly and characterized by rocky outcrops
of granite.

The problem with rain falling in high intensity storms
is that the total annual supply covers too short a period for
crops to mature. This becomes an especially important
problem in areas where there is a low total rainfall.

Over much of the country the low total amount and
seasonal character of the rainfall result in many
rivers and streams drying out completely during
the dry season. Only 30-40 per cent of the territory is reasonably well supplied with water by
nature throughout the year. Much of the remainder
is virtually uninhabitable, unless artificial water
supplies can be provided during the dry season. [11]

It is for this reason that Tanganyika's rivers do not
play an important role in the economic life of this country,
as either a means of transportation or in providing water for
irrigation and power. The Rufiji and Kagera rivers are the
only ones which are navigable. The Rufiji flows into the
Indian Ocean from the south and center of Tanganyika and is
navigable for about sixty miles by small vessels; while the
Kagera, which flows into Lake Victoria through the West
Lake Region, is similarly navigable for about ninety miles.
This situation is described by Moffett:

The lakes are in many respects of more signifi-
cance than the rivers, for the country, although
appearing well-watered on the map, has in fact
few permanent rivers of any size. This is the
natural result of a rainy season which extends,
as a rule, over less than half the year, in a
country not remarkable for the thickness of its
forest cover. During the rains there are rivers
everywhere--often so large as to present a serious problem to railway and road engineers--but
at the end of the dry season the vast majority have
dried up completely. [12]

Mineral Resources

As of now, Tanganyika does not produce in significant amounts those minerals which could provide the basis for rapid industrial growth, e. g. , iron, coal, and oil. Its two major minerals, both of which are produced solely for export, are diamonds and gold (see Table 2). Prior to 1945, gold was Tanganyika's leading produced mineral. In 1945, diamond production in value terms surpassed gold; and by 1948, it was more than double that of gold. From 1948-62, the value of diamond production increased five-fold, while that of gold did little more than double.

Tanganyika does contain mineral resources such as coal, iron ore, copper, nickel, graphite, and tungsten which could be useful in establishing an industrial base, except that they are presently economically inaccessible. For example, the Southern Highlands Region is estimated to contain in the Ngaka-Kitewaka Coal Fields 216 million tons of proved extractable coal plus an additional 40 million tons. [13] The problem involved in extracting this coal is the lack of adequate transportation facilities to carry this mineral to the market, as well as to transport heavy capital equipment to the mines. One proposal is to construct a railroad from Dar Es Salaam to Ndola in Zambia. This railway would pass through the Southern Highlands Region, thus opening it up for the development of the coal industry. Because of the high costs and long payoff period required, this project has remained in the planning stage. [14]

POPULATION RESOURCES

Composition and Growth of Population

Tanganyika has seven main racial groupings. Race is used in reference to the national origin of Tanganyika's population rather than in reference to their color. The racial groupings are: (1) European, (2) African, (3) Indian, (4) Pakistani, (5) Goan, (6) Arab, and (7) Somalis. Of these, the African population is by far the dominant group as shown in Table 3.

TABLE 2

MINERAL PRODUCTION, 1955-62

Year	Diamonds	Gold	Total	Diamonds and Gold as Per Cent of Total
	(thousands of tons)			
1955	3,199	941	5,494	75.4
1956	2,865	890	5,490	68.4
1957	3,242	793	5,441	74.2
1958	4,415	854	6,766	77.9
1959	4,548	1,197	7,199	79.8
1960	4,622	1,344	7,630	78.2
1961	5,780	1,273	7,982	88.4
1962	5,402	1,270	7,484	89.2

Source: Tanganyika, Statistical Abstract: 1963, pp. 76-77.

It is impossible to calculate accurately a rate of natural
increase for the African population because of the lack of re-
liable data on births and deaths. From 1948-65, the total
population increased by over 36 per cent, but this estimate is
based on guesses of the yearly population size. The IBRD
mission estimated that the over-all rate of natural increase
was in the vicinity of 1.75 per cent per annum, with the
Africans' and Asians' rates about 1.6 and 2.5 per cent per
year, respectively. The difference between these people's
rates is due mainly to the lower death rate of the Asians;
they reside almost entirely in cities where better medical
facilities are available.[15] The African population is estimated to have a higher birth rate than the Asians--44 per 1,000,
as compared to 35-36 per 1,000; while the Asians have a
relatively lower death rate than the Africans--9-10 per 1,000,
as compared to 25 per 1,000.[16] One of the major aims of
the Five-Year Plan is to attack infant mortality and endemic
diseases in order to increase the life expectancy of the
Africans.

Density and Geographical Distribution

While Tanganyika's over-all population density is low
relative to the United States and the United Kingdom (about
twenty-six per square mile as compared to fifty and 570,
respectively), the number of people who make their living
off of the land is too large--i.e., the land-to-labor ratio in
agriculture is low. The Economic Commission for Africa
states:

> For Africa as a whole, despite low overall densities
> for its potential agricultural areas, the populations
> can be considered as too large in relation to the
> means of subsistence obtained from the soil. This
> will cease to be true when methods of cultivation
> have progressed in a more general fashion and if
> social structures can be transformed in ways which
> will permit a faster increase of output than increase
> in population.[17]

The number of agriculturally employed males per
square mile of agricultural land is an indicator of this population pressure. While there are about sixty agriculturally

TABLE 3

POPULATION DISTRIBUTION BY RACE

Race	1948	
	Absolute (thousands)	Per Cent of Total
European	10.6	0.14
African	7,407.5	99.06
Indian-Pakistani[a]	44.2	0.59
Goan	2.0	0.02
Arab	11.1	0.15
Other[b]	2.2	0.03
Total	7,477.7	100.00

[a]There are no projected estimates of the population of the Goans. Goans are included under the Indian-Pakistani category.

[b]Projected estimates of the category "other" are significantly underestimated. In 1957, the census recorded that there were 6,900 people in this category. The projected estimates,

TABLE 3--Continued

1957		1962	
Absolute (thousands)	Per Cent of Total	Absolute (thousands)	Per Cent of Total
20.5	0.23	21.4	0.22
8,862.7	98.60	9,149.0	98.53
71.7	0.82	87.3	0.91
4.8	0.05	27.8	0.29
19.1	0.22	--b	--b
6.9	0.08	4.9	0.05
8,785.6	100.00	9,560.0	100.00

however, of this category record only 3,900 people in 1957, and 4,900 people in 1962. See Tanganyika, Statistical Abstract: 1962, pp. 10-11.

Source: Tanganyika, Statistical Abstract: 1962, Tables C.1 and C.2, pp. 10-11.

employed males per square mile in Tanganyika, [18] the number is only about three in the United States. [19]

The four most heavily populated regions are: (1) Lake,
(2) West Lake, (3) Tanga, and (4) Eastern. Three of these--
Lake, West Lake, and Tanga--are also three of the most
fertile areas. The Eastern Region is relatively heavily populated mainly because it includes Tanganyika's principle city--
Dar Es Salaam.

The fastest growing regions, with respect to population,
are Tanga, Lake, and Northern. These three regions are
also the areas where the greatest amount of agricultural production for cash occurs. The Tanga Region is the main sisal
producing area; the Northern contains the major coffee producing districts, while the Lake is Tanganyika's main cotton
producing region. The three slowest growing regions, on the
other hand, are the Central, Western, and Southern. The
Central is the driest, while the Western and Southern are
infested with the tsetse fly. It should be noted that, while
the Central Region has a larger percentage of its area classified as agricultural than the national average, it is Tanganyika's slowest growing region. A probable explanation is that,
given its present supply of water, its agricultural limit has
been reached.

Most of Tanganyika's population lives in rural areas.
Only 3.5 per cent live in towns of 5,000 and above (see Table
4), as compared to 34.0 per cent of the world's population
living in urban areas of 20,000 and above in the 1950's. [20]
The Europeans and Asians are by comparison town dwellers--
e.g., around 43 per cent of the Europeans and 75 per cent of
the Asians in 1957 lived in towns of 5,000 or above. On the
other hand, only 2.7 per cent of the Africans lived in these
towns; by and large, the Africans still live in rural tribal
areas. Table 5 lists the major tribes, with the sizes of their
respective populations.

From 1948 to 1957, the town population grew at a faster
rate than the total population--7.1 per cent as compared to
1.6 per cent. The growth of urban areas in Tanganyika is
likely on balance to have a positive effect on this country's
rate of economic growth. Cities serve to: (1) weaken tribal
ties, (2) increase the spread of new ideas, and (3) provide

TABLE 4

THE SIZE OF THE TOWNS
IN TANGANYIKA, 1957

Name of Town	Size (thousands)	As a Percentage of the Total Population Living in Towns of More than 5,000 People
Dar Es Salaam	128.7	41.8
Tanga	38.1	12.4
Mwanza	19.9	6.5
Tabora	15.4	5.0
Morogoro	14.5	4.7
Moshi	13.7	4.5
Dodoma	13.4	4.4
Ujiji	12.0	3.9
Mtwana	10.5	3.4
Lindi	10.3	3.3
Arusha	10.0	3.2
Iringa	9.6	3.1
Mbeya	6.9	2.2
Mikindana	4.8	1.6
Total	307.8	

Source: Tanganyika, Statistical Abstract: 1962, p. 16.

TABLE 5

THE SIZE OF THE MAIN TRIBES
OF TANGANYIKA, 1957

Name of Tribe	Absolute Size (thousands)	Relative Size (per cent)
Sukuma	1,093.4	12.6
Nyamwezi	362.8	4.2
Makonde	333.9	3.9
Haya	325.4	3.8
Chagga	318.2	3.7
Gogo	299.4	3.5
Ha	289.8	3.3
Hehe	251.6	2.9
Nyakusa	219.7	2.5
Lugurw	202.3	2.3
Bena	195.8	2.3
Turw	195.7	2.3
Sambaa	193.8	2.2
Zaramo	183.3	2.1
Iramba	156.5	1.8
Yao	144.2	1.7
Mwera	138.2	1.6
Iragw	135.1	1.6
Zigua	134.4	1.6
Pare	126.0	1.5
Makua	123.3	1.4
Nyika	122.2	1.4
Rangi	110.3	1.3
Other Tribes	3,007.2	34.7
Total	8,662.7	100.0

Source: Tanganyika, Statistical Abstract: 1962.

a concentrated market for goods and resources.[21] Cities, however, are not costless. The growth of employment opportunities in the cities has not kept pace with the growth of its population. In Dar Es Salaam this has led to a serious unemployment problem,[22] and subsequently to political unrest.

The government, with little success, has attempted to induce these unemployed Africans to resettle on the land.[23] Recently, the government has adopted a more forceful method--banishment from the cities with a jail sentence as punishment if they return.[24] In addition, cities induce extra expenditures on such forms of social overhead capital as houses, public buildings, electricity, etc., which result in a diversion of capital funds from more productive opportunities.

Employment Characteristics

The age data is highly inaccurate, because of such factors in census counts as memory lapses, illiteracy of census respondents, and general suspicion by the native African toward any kind of enumeration.[25] On the basis of the available data, the age structures of the African and Asian populations appear to be skewed toward the younger age groups. Table 6 indicates the pyramidal age structure of the African segment of the population. The major economic problem caused by such an age distribution is the large dependency ratio, i.e., the large number of nonproductive workers which must be supported by the productive labor.[26] The young people must be fed, even though they do not contribute much to the gross domestic product and may die before they do.[27]

Wage Employment

Tanganyika's work force is characterized by a low degree of occupational specialization.[28] An indicator is the small percentage of Tanganyika's people engaged in paid employment; it amounts to about 5 per cent of the total population, as shown in Table 7.

It is difficult to measure accurately the total number of people who engage in paid employment during the year because the yearly estimates are based on the enumeration

TABLE 6

THE AGE STRUCTURE OF THE AFRICAN
POPULATION OF TANGANYIKA, 1957

Age Group	Per Cent	Number (thousands)
0-9	31.0	2,682
10-19	22.3	1,934
20-29	17.5	1,510
30-39	12.9	1,116
40-49	8.5	733
50-59	5.0	434
60 and over	3.5	299

Source: Tanganyika, Statistical Abstract: 1962, Tables
C.8(a) and C.8(b).

TABLE 7

PAID EMPLOYEES BY INDUSTRIAL
DIVISION, 1964

Industrial Division	Number of Employees	Per Cent of Total Employees
Agriculture, Forestry and Fishing	153,410	43.7
Mining and Quarrying	7,755	2.2
Manufacturing	22,594	6.4
Building and Construction	11,541	3.3
Electricity and Water	1,820	0.5
Commerce	17,341	4.9
Transport and Communications	9,344	2.7
Private Services	23,651	6.7
Public Services	103,801	29.6
Total	351,257	100.0

Source: Budget Survey 1965-66 (Dar Es Salaam: Government Printer, 1965), p. 27.

conducted on a particular date, while many Africans are only
temporarily engaged in paid employment during the year.[29]
The number of Africans who work for wages during the year
is then a multiple of the number employed on any given date.
There is a constant shift of workers between jobs in urban
areas and work on subsistence and cash crops in rural areas,
as well as between peasant farming and jobs on estates and
in mines.[30] The major percentage of the migrants spend only
about six to eighteen months in paid employment before returning to their rural homes, although three to six months away
is not unusual. As to the magnitude of internal migration,
there are no accurate estimates of the total number involved.
Gulliver estimates that approximately one third of the total
labor force are migrant workers.[31]

The major causes of internal migration are mainly
economic. First, the African migrants need cash to: (1)
purchase food to supplement their subsistence output, (2)
pay taxes, (3) buy specific nonfood items such as bicycles,
radios, etc., and (4) purchase certain types of capital equipment, e.g., ploughs.[32] Secondly, the British discouraged
permanent settlement by the Africans in urban areas by per-
mitting them to live only in outlying areas of the cities.[33]
Thirdly, the Africans are forced to return each year to their
tribal homes in order to cultivate their land because possession is based upon its continual use. Since the natives cannot
sell their land, they are unable to realize the capitalized
value of their farms; and in effect, if they abandon their tribe,
they are taxed a part of their wealth.[34] And lastly, the tribal
areas with their close kinship ties are viewed by the Africans
as an old age security system.[35]

From this it appears that the political leaders are
faced with a dilemma. While they have too many people in
the city at any one time, these Africans are not permanently
settled; and thus they do not have the incentive to learn industrial skills and discipline. This problem can only be
solved through the general development of the economy which
will provide a large increase in the number of attractive jobs.
The existence of such opportunities at wage employment
centers will induce many Africans to terminate their tribal
attachments and form permanent attachments to wage jobs.
On the other hand, the existence of an unskilled, undisciplined

work force is itself an impediment to such economic development.

Literacy and Education

The number of illiterate Africans in Tanganyika is substantial.[36] The Economic Commission for Africa estimates
that only 5 to 10 per cent of Tanganyika's adult population
was literate in 1950,[37] while Betty George of the United
States Department of Health, Education, and Welfare estimates that only 16 per cent of the African children of school
age were attending school.[38] Tanganyika's educational system consists mainly of primary schools. In 1961, there
were 506,260 Africans enrolled in 3,238 primary schools;
this accounts for about 98 per cent of the African public
schools and African students.[39]

Tanganyika's primary manpower goal is to become
self-sufficient, except for some highly specialized jobs, by
1980. The planners estimate that their development needs
for the Five-Year Plan are: (1) 3,200 people with university
degrees, (2) 9,300 people with two years post-secondary
education or training, e.g., school teachers, engineering
technicians, etc., and (3) 16,000 people with a secondary
education such as clerks, skilled craftsmen, etc.[40]

Since Tanganyika has mainly emphasized primary education up to 1961, as noted above, the main shortage of
educational facilities is in secondary and university education. In 1961, there were only forty-two secondary schools
with a total enrollment of 6,031 students, and 598 students
with a higher university education;[41] this can be compared to
over 500,000 students in primary.[42] From July, 1962, to
June, 1967, the secondary school enrollment was expected to
increase to 24,300, which amounts to an increase of over
300 per cent.[43] The government allocated 45 per cent of its
educational expenditure in the Three-Year Plan to increasing
and improving the facilities of secondary schools,[44] and over
85 per cent of its educational expenditure in the Five-Year
Plan to secondary, technical, and higher education.[45] The
major part of the finance, however, is expected to come
from foreign sources. For example, the International Development Association, an affiliate of the IBRD, extended

credit equivalent to Ł1, 640, 000 (total government expenditure on capital improvement in the Five-Year Plan amounts
only to Ł14, 000). These funds are to be used to create new
secondary educational facilities for 6, 900 students. [46] The
major governmental expense lies in recurrent expenditures;
in this area, the Peace Corps is aiding in covering the present shortage of teachers.

Education cannot serve as a panacea for all of Tanganyika's problems. While it is necessary to have a skilled
labor force to attract industry to this country and to administer the provision of the plan, a major problem in facilitat-
ing secondary and university education[47] is whether the benefits received are worth the costs. In promoting agricultural
change, there are serious drawbacks to relying too heavily
on education. First there is a snob effect. Persons with
education, especially university, often tend to view the
peasant farmers with contempt, and to concentrate their
development efforts on the cities. Secondly, and related to
the first, these people do not desire to work with the peasant
farmers, the area where education is most necessary. Graduates desire to secure government positions which will keep
them in Dar Es Salaam. [48] And thirdly, the knowledge of
college graduates is often too advanced to be useful in aiding
the peasant to increase his agricultural production. Nyerere
stated at an FAO conference, in Rome, on November 18,
1963, that the major problem with the use of FAO experts is
that they were ". . . too expert to be useful. " He noted,
'"What we need very badly are practical men who know their
job and who will come and work with our people while they
train them. . . . "[49]

This is not to suggest that education does not play a
useful role in development. Health expenditures to eliminate
debilitating diseases, as well as educational expenditures,
are investments in human capital, which yield a rate of return. The point is that, like all other forms of investment,
there is an opportunity cost involved; and overinvestment can
easily occur if the view is adopted that education is the main
key to development.

In conclusion, Tanganyika cannot be characterized as
a rich nation with respect to its natural and population

resources. It has a small percentage of its land classified as agricultural, because of rainfall conditions, tsetse fly, and nature of the soil. The presently economically accessible minerals are not those which will provide Tanganyika with an industrial base. The age structure of the population is skewed toward the young, while the work force can be generally classified as lacking skills and stability. While education is a necessary ingredient in order for workers to acquire new skills, investments which create high paying jobs are needed to attach labor permanently to wage-earning employment and to induce them to learn new skills.

CHAPTER **2** GOVERNMENTAL
PLANNING

In Tanganyika the role of initiating economic activity is more the responsibility of the government planners than of private entrepreneurs. As stated before, the political leaders hold the view that the private sector has failed to generate a satisfactory rate of economic growth in the past, or to ensure an equitable distribution of the national wealth between Africans and non-Africans; and given the present conditions in Tanganyika, it is unlikely to do so in the future.

The aim of the political leaders is to use planning as a method of achieving a rapid change in the present nature of the economic system. There are two goals, as stated previously: (1) under government auspicies the mobilization and allocation of resources into those projects which will lead to a substantially higher rate of economic growth, and (2) the Africanization of all decision-making positions both in the private and public sectors. The type of planning currently being used is not a replica of that used in the Communist world. The procedures do not call for the complete elimination of the private sector, at least at this time, but rather for the direction of effort into private activities along those lines which will be most beneficial in achieving their two goals.

THE MEANING OF ECONOMIC PLANNING

Tanganyika's government officials have considered three types of planning as means to achieve their national objectives: (1) capital budgeting, which was used from 1961-64; (2) comprehensive economic planning, which is currently being used; and (3) central planning, which some government officials desire to experiment with in the distant future. Capital budgeting and comprehensive economic planning involve planned governmental expenditures aimed at increasing the resource base and rate of capital formation of the country.

28

It includes only governmental expenditures--directly on
projects, or indirectly by encouraging private investment on
projects which lead to the formation of capital--without
specifying targets of production increases for sectors of the
economy. Comprehensive economic planning not only involves specifying targets of production increases for sectors,
but also includes the planned investment expenditures of the
private and public sectors.)

    Central planning differs from both of the above in that
it involves the complete direction by the government of all
economic activity. Besides the direction of savings into
measures which lead to capital accumulation and to resource
expansion, this would include the allocation and management
of all resources used during the year for consumption and
investment purposes.[2] In most of the nations of Africa today,
this type of planning is not used.[3]

CAPITAL BUDGETING: 1961/62-1963/64

    The Three-Year Development Plan (1961/62-1963/64)[4]
amounted to a capital budget. Planning did not involve the
complete governmental administration of all phases of economic activity; nor did it even involve the stating of specific
growth rates for the economy, or the attainment of target
increases in production in certain sectors by certain dates.
The Development planners stated in this connection:

        The reality of economic planning in the hustle and
        bustle of a fast developing African country bears
        little or no relation to the theoretical work on
        elegant models constructed in statistical labora-
        tories of more developed countries. In Tanganyika,
        it has not even proved possible to follow the "pro-
        gramming" approach which starts from over-all
        targets of gross domestic product and estimates
        subsequently the resulting levels of consumption,
        imports, exports, capital formation, and other
        relevant aggregates.[5]

    The planners' aim was to broaden the economy's base
through a concentrated investment program in certain designated areas of economic activity. The political leaders

stated that the economy could be given its greatest boost by
channelling funds into a limited number of projects. The
areas decided upon were: (1) the development of livestock
and agricultural production including water development and
irrigation, (2) the construction of a trunk road system, and
(3) the development of secondary and technical education. [6]
This is indicated in Table 8.

The government immediately encountered administrative problems in implementing the plan's provisions. The
target funds were not spent in any of the years in which the
plan was in operation (see Table 9). The reasons given were
a lack of a qualified staff to establish and manage the projects, and delays in obtaining overseas funds. [7] Despite
these administrative problems, the government adopted a
more complex and more ambitious form of planning in 1964.

COMPREHENSIVE ECONOMIC
PLANNING: 1964-69

On May 13, 1964, Julius Nyerere announced that there
were to be three Five-Year Plans running consecutively
from 1964-80. [8] By 1980, it is hoped to achieve the following goals: (1) to raise per capita income from £19.6 to
£45, (2) to make Tanganyika self-sufficient with respect to
trained manpower, and (3) to raise the life expectancy from
thirty-five to between forty and fifty years. [9]

The first of these Five-Year Plans is to run from
1964-69, and its aim is to raise per capita income to about
£30 by 1970 as well as to prepare the groundwork for the
achievement of the other two goals. [10] In order to achieve
these short-run goals, the plan includes target rates of increases for the economy as a whole, as well as for sectors
(see Table 10). These rates of increase indicate that the
government is hoping to speed up the growth process considerably.

The adoption of this type of planning involves a change
in attitude as to what is possible in the way of planning. In
framing the Three-Year Plan, the government admitted that
it was impossible, given the lack of data as well as the unreliability of the available data, to engage in a sophisticated

TABLE 8

DEVELOPMENT PLAN
1961/62-1963/64

| Ministry | Expenditure | |
	Amount (£ thousands)	Per Cent
Government--Central and Local[a]	4,676	19.5
Agriculture	5,737	24.0
Communications, Power and Works[b]	6,900	28.8
Education	3,270	13.7
Commerce and Industry	1,095	4.6
Health and Labor	954	4.0
Lands and Surveys	1,298	5.4
Total	23,930	100.0

[a]Includes expenditure by Ministry of Local Government, Office of the Prime Minister, and Ministry of Home Affairs-- e.g., prisons.

[b]Planned expenditure on water development and irrigation and on a trunk road system was £2,291,000 or 9.6 per cent of the total, and £3,217,000 or 13.5 per cent of the totals, respectively.

Source: Development Plan, 1961/62-1963/64, Table XIII, p. 13.

TABLE 9

PLANNED AND ACTUAL DEVELOPMENT
EXPENDITURES, 1961/62-1963/64

Year	Planned Expenditure £ thousands	Actual Expenditure £ thousands	Per Cent (Actual ÷ Planned)
1961/62	7,977	7,341	92.0
1962/63	7,977	5,674	71.1
1963/64	7,977	7,263	91.1
Total	23,930[a]	20,278	84.7

[a]Column may not add up to total because of rounding.

Source: Development Plan, 1961/62-1963/64, pp. 13-14;
         Tanganyika, Budget Survey 1964-65 (Dar Es Salaam:
         Government Printer, 1964), p. 18; and Tanganyika,
         Budget Survey 1965-66 (Dar Es Salaam: Government
         Printer, 1965), p. 37.

TABLE 10

ACTUAL AND PLANNED RATES OF INCREASES
FOR THE ECONOMY AND SECTORS,
1954-61 AND 1964-69

	Planned Per Cent Increases, 1964-69	Actual Per Cent Increases, 1954-61[a]
Economy		
National Income	6.7	4.5
Population	2.2	1.8
Per Capita Income	4.6	2.7
Sector		
Crop Husbandry	4.8	2.7
Subsistence	2.0	1.9
Marketed	7.5	3.5
Processing and Manufacturing	14.8	5.8
Commerce	8.0	7.7
Construction	12.7	1.7
Transportation and Communication	7.8	6.2
Public Utilities	12.3	18.3

[a]Rates include price rises.

Source: Five-Year Plan 1964-69, pp. 8-10.

form of planning. The data have been little improved since
the writing of the Three-Year Plan, and the present attempt
can be questioned as being too ambitious. As it will be
pointed out later in this study, it appears that these target
increases listed in Table 9 are goals, based on hopes, rather
than realistic projections.

The plan calls for a total investment by both private
investors and government of Ł 246,000,000 during the five-
year period. The planned public expenditure is Ł130,000,000.
If the planned investment were equally divided among the
five years, this would amount to a yearly expenditure of
Ł 26,000,000, which is larger than that of the whole Three-
Year Plan. The total planned expenditure of the Three-Year
Plan was about Ł 24,000,000. [11]

The private sector is expected to invest about
Ł 116,000,000 during this same period. This figure, however, remains a rather tentative estimate because of the
lack of direct governmental control over investment decisions.
As Mr. A. Z. N. Swai states:

> In the Public Sector the policies for the achievement
> of targets will be those of direction of effort and of
> organizing the necessary supplies of manpower,
> finance and materials, while in the Private Sector
> they will be rather those of instilling confidence in
> the private investor and creating an economic cli-
> mate conducive to investment. [12]

Table 11 shows a breakdown of public and private expenditure by activity.

The major change in the Five-Year Plan is the increased emphasis on industrial development. This is shown
in Table 12. The major reason given by the Planning Division is that agricultural production, viewed from the long
run, is an unattractive industry to rely upon for the future
expansion of economic activity. The Division of Planning
fears that the world market for agricultural produce will be
relatively smaller in twenty years or so than it is today, i.e.,
the planners are forecasting that rising productivity in primary producing countries, plus the additional number of
peasant farmers who will begin to produce for the market,

TABLE 11

EXPENDITURES IN CAPITAL FORMATION
PROJECTS BY THE PUBLIC AND
PRIVATE SECTORS, 1964-69

Sector	Expenditures (£ millions)		
	Public	Private	Total
Agriculture	28.5	8.4	36.9
Industry	14.6	41.7	56.3
Commerce	3.6	29.5	33.1
Economic Infrastructure[a]	39.3	2.7	42.0
Social Infrastructure[b]	36.2	33.7	69.9
Administration	7.8	--	7.8
Total	130.0	116.0	246.0

[a]Includes: (1) Roads, (2) Railways and Harbors, and (3) Power.

[b]Includes: (1) Housing and Township Development, (2) Community Development, (3) Education, and (4) Health and Welfare.

Source: Five-Year Plan 1964-69, p. 91.

TABLE 12

GOVERNMENT EXPENDITURE,
1961-69

Sector	1961/62-1963/64 (per cent)	1964-69 (per cent)
Agriculture, Livestock, Forestry, and Irrigation	25.1	21.9
Industry and Commerce	4.2	14.0
Economic Infrastructure	25.9[a]	30.2
Social Infrastructure	28.0	27.8
Government Services	14.8	6.0[b]
Total	100.0	100.0

[a]Excludes Railroads and Harbors.

[b]Such services as the preservation of wildlife, information services, etc., now included under Recurrent Expenditures.

Source: Development Plan 1961/62-1963/64, p. 14; and
Five-Year Plan 1964-69, p. 91.

will increase the world supply of primary produce at a faster
rate than the total demand of developed nations can increase.
The result will be a continual deterioration in the terms of
trade of primary producing nations. In this study, it will be
pointed out that any attempt at industrial diversification without an agricultural revolution is unlikely to be successful.

In addition, there are two major administrative problems in carrying out the provisions of this plan. In light of
the failure of the government to meet its planned yearly development expenditure under the Tree-Year Plan, the com-
mitment imposed by this Five-Year Plan seems rather over-
ambitious. The government has already announced that many
of the projects planned for the first year of the new plan have
had to be carried over to the second year;[13] and the annual
expenditure is supposed to increase each year (see Table 13).

Secondly, the government appears to be relying rather
heavily on admonition and feelings of patriotism in order to
achieve the objectives of the plan, rather than solely economic
incentives; in fact, there is an air of militancy surrounding
its implementation, as is indicated in the speech of Julius
Nyerere introducing the plan to the members of Parliament.

> To achieve the objectives of the Development Plan
> the whole nation must work as a team. We must
> marshall all the help we can get for our struggle.
> And, in working for the future, we must guard all
> that is valuable in our inheritance. . . On the land,
> in the factories, in the classroom, in the hospitals;
> all of us; politicians, civil servants, soldiers,
> policemen, men, women, and children, let us say:
> 'It can be done, play your part. '[14]

No one who has read the works of Julius Nyerere can doubt
for an instant his unselfishness and self-sacrifice in attempting to create a better life for Tanganyika's people. On the
other hand, such an approach is likely to lead to a divergence
between the private and social good, if each peasant con-
siders the private rewards to be less than the social gain.
In this case the effort that the African may offer to achieve
the plan's goals will be less than that which is considered to
be socially desirable.

TABLE 13

TOTAL DEVELOPMENT EXPENDITURE OF
THE CENTRAL GOVERNMENT PER YEAR,
1964/65-1968/69

Year	Planned Central Government Expenditures (£ thousands)
1964/65	14,902
1965/66	16,885
1966/67	19,767
1967/68	23,954
1968/69	26,492
Total	102,000

Source: Five-Year Plan 1964-69, p. 93.

The problem is: Can the political leaders achieve their
goals of a high rate of economic growth and a rapid rate of
Africanization? Even though the data currently available in
Tanganyika are lacking and unreliable, it is possible to examine the present economic system with respect to the
nature and size of the problems which the planners face. By
then noting the methods which the planners are using to solve
these problems, some tentative conclusions can be made.

CHAPTER **3** A STATISTICAL
EXAMINATION OF THE
ECONOMIC SYSTEM

This chapter deals with the nature and level of economic activity in Tanganyika. Its purpose is to describe statistically the structure of the economy and to point out the main obstacles to its rapid change. This chapter is divided into two parts for discussion purposes. Part One deals with the conceptual and statistical problems involved in measuring economic activity. Part Two is concerned with the present level of economic activity, the size of the public sector, and the obstacles within the economic system to governmental policies designed to promote industrialization.

PROBLEMS IN THE STATISTICAL
MEASUREMENT OF ECONOMIC ACTIVITY

There are two basic problems in measuring the changes in the level of economic activity in Tanganyika: (1) there have been procedural changes in the collection of national output data, and (2) there are conceptual and statistical difficulties in collecting data on economic activity in the indigenous sector. The terms indigenous and subsistence are synonomous.

PROCEDURAL CHANGES

The national accounts of Tanganyika indicate the size and source of the gross domestic product at factor cost. The gross domestic product at factor cost is defined as the total value of all goods and services produced within the borders of a country during a specified time--usually one year. It is determined by summing the value added in each process of production, i.e., it is calculated by deducting from the gross value of all production the output of each industry which is used in the production of other goods. [1]

Estimates of the gross domestic product of Tanganyika are available for the years 1952-64. Alan T. Peacock and Douglas G. M. Dosser provide estimates for the years 1952-54, while the government statisticians provide them for the years 1954-64. Because of differences in calculation procedures, the government's estimates are lower than those of Peacock and Dosser; and, thus, these two series are not comparable. [2]

The government estimates of gross domestic product from 1963 on are not comparable with earlier estimates, ". . . as the definition of the various sectors of the economy, and the methods of calculating some of the figures have been changed from those adopted in earlier series."[3] The government did recalculate its estimates for the years 1960-62, but this still leaves three series of figures which are not comparable: 1952-54, 1954-62, and 1960-64. Since the sectors are identical in the first two series, these are presented as one in Table 14. Table 15 presents the third series separately.

CONCEPTUAL AND STATISTICAL PROBLEMS

In estimating the gross domestic product of any under-developed country, the first conceptual problem which must be solved lies in defining the nature of the firm. In a nation such as Tanganyika, the household is commonly both the production and consumption unit. The family households of Tanganyika provide most of the services which are normally purchased by households attached to a monetary market. Such services as the storing and marketing of goods, the manufacture of household utensils and clothing, the processing of raw materials, etc., are supplied by the household members, rather than by specialized agencies as in a market economy. The exclusion of these nonmarketed services from gross domestic product estimates, unlike the situation in a developed country, would lead to a serious underestimation of the level of economic activity in an African country, because a large percentage of total economic activity is performed in this way.

A. R. Prest and I. G. Stewart argued on conceptual grounds that intrahousehold services should be included in estimates of gross domestic product in African countries. The relationship among household members is a commercial one,

TABLE 14

TANGANYIKA'S GROSS DOMESTIC PRODUCT
AT FACTOR COST, 1952-62
(millions of pounds)

Sector	1952[a]	1953[a]	1954	1955
Agriculture	66.3	64.8	68.3	72.5
Livestock Products	10.4	13.7	13.3	12.7
Forest Products	5.2	5.7	5.1	5.3
Hunting and Fishing	1.3	1.4	1.4	1.5
Mining and Quarrying	2.1	2.3	4.6	5.1
Manufacturing	5.0	4.4	3.8	4.1
Craft Industries	5.5	5.6	5.2	5.3
Construction[b]	11.2	10.7	10.5	8.1
Public Utilities	0.4	0.5	0.7	0.8
Transport, Storage, and Communications	7.9	7.6	8.0	8.5
Distribution	9.0	10.1	7.0	7.6
Ownership of Dwellings	2.2	2.4	2.6	2.7
Public Administration and Defense	5.6	7.2	7.7	8.7
Miscellaneous Services	2.8	3.1	3.6	4.0
	(134.9)[c]	(139.5)[c]		
Total	129.9[d]	135.4[d]	141.7	146.3

[a]Estimates of Alan T. Peacock and Douglas G. M. Dosser, p. 45.

[b]Peacock and Dosser call this sector "building and civil engineering." The National Income of Tanganyika 1952-54, p. 45.

[c]Estimates of gross domestic product at market price.

[d]Estimates of gross domestic product at factor cost. Taxes on expenditure (5.0 million pounds for 1952 and 4.1 million

TABLE 14--Continued

1956	1957	1958	1959	1960	1961	1962[e]
74.4	76.5	75.1	80.0	82.5	80.1	91.8
12.9	14.6	15.0	16.7	18.4	17.2	17.4
5.7	6.0	5.3	5.1	5.0	4.7	4.5
1.7	2.1	2.9	3.4	3.6	3.7	4.0
5.0	5.0	6.2	6.6	7.0	7.3	6.8
4.0	5.7	6.8	7.1	7.5	7.7	8.5
5.3	5.6	5.7	5.8	5.9	6.0	6.1
9.3	10.3	10.5	10.0	10.9	12.9	12.7
0.9	0.6	1.0	1.1	1.1	1.4	1.5
9.0	10.2	11.4	12.3	13.3	13.9	14.2
7.6	7.7	7.8	8.6	8.6	8.3	8.3
2.9	3.1	3.3	3.5	3.7	4.0	4.1
9.3	10.4	11.3	11.8	13.3	15.7	17.3
4.3	4.5	4.8	5.2	5.4	5.8	6.0
152.4	162.4	167.1	177.1	186.2	188.7	203.3

pounds for 1953) have been subtracted from gross domestic product at market prices to gain this estimate. The National Income of Tanganyika 1952-54, p. 45.

[e]Preliminary estimates.

Source: Gross Domestic Product of Tanganyika 1954-57, p. 4; Tanganyika, Statistical Abstract: 1960, p. 123; Tanganyika, Statistical Abstract: 1962, p. 138; The National Income of Tanganyika 1952-54, p. 45; and Tanganyika, Budget Survey 1963-64 (Dar Es Salaam: Government Printer, 1963), p. 3.

TABLE 15

TANGANYIKA'S GROSS DOMESTIC PRODUCT
AT FACTOR COST, 1960-64
(₤ millions)

Sector	1960	1961	1962	1963	1964
Agriculture	112.8	114.1	124.3	138.7	140.6
Mining and					
Quarrying	5.2	5.4	5.1	4.4	5.9
Manufacturing	5.3	7.0	7.7	8.1	8.7
Construction	4.6	5.8	6.1	6.4	7.5
Electricity and					
Water	1.2	1.4	1.5	1.5	1.7
Commerce	20.9	22.2	24.2	26.9	28.4
Rent	8.0	8.4	8.8	9.4	11.1
Transport	8.7	8.6	9.3	9.4	10.0
Services	18.1	20.6	21.6	27.6	30.3
Total	185.1	193.5	208.6	232.3	244.3

Source: Tanganyika, Budget Survey 1965-66 (Dar Es Salaam:
Government Printer, 1965), p. 4.

unlike that in households of developed nations;[4] for example, wife rights, which include work rights, are acquired through the payment of material goods, called bride-price, and compensation can be gained for violation of these rights. [5]

Peacock and Dosser disagreed, however, with this line of reasoning on grounds that it was no more compelling to include these services in the accounts of African countries than it is in developed countries. [6] From the above discussion, this opinion appears weak. The major drawback, on the other hand, to including these statistics is the difficulties involved in gathering such data; and consequently, the results may not justify the costs. While government statisticians do not measure the value of nonmarket household services separately, part of the value of these services are included in estimates of the gross domestic product. Since the value of such output as crop production is estimated, the value of the services which contribute to it are implicitly included. [7]

Another statistical problem is uncovered in attempting to collect data on the nature and size of subsistence output. In the monetary part of the economy information on output is furnished as a by-product of the recorded sales of goods and services. In the subsistence part, however, there are no transactions of sales to be recorded, by definition, because the producer consumes his own output. Thus lack of statistical sources has led to the government's making subjective estimates of production by family households for personal consumption. Some examples are crop and meat output, hut building, and beer.

Estimates of subsistence crop production are made by agricultural officers. These estimates are based on: (1) estimated consumption per head, (2) diets, (3) estimates of calorie intake, (4) estimates of acreage under cultivation, and (5) an adjustment of estimates of previous years' outputs in light of population growth, famine conditions, etc. [8] C. J. Martin, in commenting on the national accounts of Tanganyika, noted that the most serious limitation in using this procedure was that yearly fluctuations of income can easily be the result of changes in personnel making the estimates. [9]

Estimates of subsistence meat production are made by veterinary officers. These estimates are based on: (1)

estimated reproduction rates, (2) the total number of hides
and skins imported, and (3) dietary surveys. Estimates of
African hut building in rural areas are based on population
data. The 1949 census is used as the base year, adjusted by
the data collected in the 1957 census. On the basis of these
data, estimates of the total number of African huts are made
on the assumption that each adult male owns one house. The
most important item produced by the cottage industry is
homebrew. Estimates of total output are made on the assumption that each adult male consumes one gallon of this beer--
known as "pombe"--per week. [10] In spite of these serious
weaknesses in the data, the statistics can still be used as a
valuable indicator of the nature of the economy's structure
and of obstacles to rapid changes.

THE STRUCTURE OF THE ECONOMIC SYSTEM

Indicators of Economic Growth

Income statistics are used as an aid in comparing the
levels of living of nations. The phrase "level of living" is
herein defined as those living conditions which the people of
a nation are actually experiencing. This phrase differs in
meaning from the phrase "standard of living" which is herein
defined as the living conditions to which people aspire or are
hoping to enjoy. [11] One of the main statistical indicators
used in measuring levels of living is per capita income.

The per capita income level of Tanganyika is very low,
compared to the United States and the United Kingdom. Table
16 shows the differences in per capita income levels among
the United States, the United Kingdom, Tanganyika, Kenya,
and Uganda, for the year 1964.

These per capita income statistics do not accurately
measure the relative level of living of the people of Tanganyika, i.e., it cannot be said, on the basis of these statistics,
that the people of the United States enjoy an average level of
living fifty-five times greater than that of the people of Tanganyika. There are two problems which arise in converting
currencies of different nations into a common one: (1) different goods and services produced in each of these countries,

TABLE 16

PER CAPITA INCOME, 1964
(current dollars)

Country	Per Capita Income
United States[a]	3305.00
United Kingdom[a]	1673.00
Kenya[b]	85.45
Uganda[b]	77.10
Tanganyika[b]	58.99

[a]Income statistics of the United States and the United Kingdom are estimates of gross domestic product at market prices.

[b]Income statistics of Tanganyika, Uganda, and Kenya are estimates of gross domestic product at factor cost.

Source: United Nations, Department of Economic and Social Affairs, Statistical Yearbook: 1965; and Budget Survey 1965-66.

and (2) a lack of equivalence between the exchange rate and
the relationship of internal prices.

As to "(1)," the problem lies in attempting to measure
and compare the utility gained by people of different nations
through their expenditures when the type and quality of items
produced and consumed are different. The purchases of
people vary, not only because of variations in levels of income, but also because of differences in tastes, diets, habits,
traditions, etc. These differences in tastes, etc., condition
the preferences of people, and, in turn, these tastes, etc.,
are conditioned by the society and physical environment in
which they live. [12]

As to "(2)," a lack of equivalence between the exchange
rate and the relationship of internal prices is caused by two
factors: (2) exchange controls cause a distortion between exchange rates and internal prices, and (b) certain goods and
services are not sold on the international market, so that it
is impossible to compare the value of (say) housing which may
differ in quality from one country to another. [13]

For these reasons, per capita income statistics are
used solely as a rough indicator of the relative low living
level of Tanganyika as compared to other nations. Peacock
and Dosser state, in this connection: "Taking the comparison
for what it is worth, that is as some sort of rough guide to
living conditions. . . Now, no one would deny that these figures indicate a relatively low standard of living, even if
there is some evidence of improving conditions and even allowing for the qualifications which preface our estimates. "[14]

Per capita income statistics can also be used as an
indicator of the rate of economic growth. The annual average
rate of increase of Tanganyika's real per capita income was
approximately 2.25 per cent and 1.37 per cent from 1954-62
and from 1960-64, respectively (see Tables 17 and 18). The
large difference in the rate of economic growth between these
two time periods is partly explained by the use of 1954 as the
base year in the first series. Poor economic conditions were
experienced during the year 1954; and if 1955 is used as the
base year, the yearly increase is only 1.75 per cent. Regardless of which of the rates is used, the indication is that an un-
usually high level of per capita income has not been achieved.

TABLE 17

THE RATE OF CHANGE OF REAL
PER CAPITA INCOME, 1954-62

Year	Gross Domestic Product at Factor Cost (Ł millions)	Price Index[a]	Popula- tion (thousands)	Real Per Capita Income Column 2÷ Column 3/ Column 4 (Ł)	Per Cent Change
1954	141.7	117.6	8,304	14.5	+5.5
1955	146.7	113.9	8,454	15.3	+3.3
1956	152.4	112.3	8,605	15.8	+0.6
1957	162.4	116.7	8,759	15.9	-3.8
1958	167.2	122.4	8,916	15.3	+5.9
1959	177.1	120.5	8,076	16.2	+2.5
1960	186.2	121.5	9,237	16.6	-1.8
1961	188.7	122.6	9,421	16.3	+6.1
1962	203.3	122.5	9,607	17.3	____

Average Rate   2.25

[a]The price index, which is used, is the "Dar Es Salaam,
Retail Price Index of Goods Mainly Consumed by Africans."
The base year is 1951. This index is based on a survey of
lower-paid African workers in Dar Es Salaam. The Gross
Domestic Product of Tanganyika 1954-57, p. 29.

Source: The National Income of Tanganyika 1952-54, p. 45;
The Gross Domestic Product of Tanganyika 1954-57,
p. 4; Tanganyika, Statistical Abstract: 1960, p. 123;
Tanganyika, Statistical Abstract: 1962, p. 138; and
Budget Survey 1963-64, p. 3.

TABLE 18

THE RATE OF CHANGE OF REAL
PER CAPITA INCOME, 1960-64

Year	Gross Domestic Product at Factor Cost (Constant Pounds)[a] (thousands of dollars)	Population (thousands)	Real Per Capita Income Column 2÷ Column 3	Per Cent Change
1960	185,053	9,237	20.0	-6.0
1961	177,192	9,421	18.8	+5.3
1962	189,809	9,607	19.8	+2.0
1963	197,538	9,798	20.2	+4.5
1964	210,462	9,990	21.1	
			Average Rate	1.38

[a]Estimates are in terms of 1960 pounds.

Source: Budget Survey 1965-66, p. 5.

At an annual rate of increase of 2.0 per cent, it would take
about twenty-five years for the level of per capita income to
reach $100 U.S.

In calculating real per capita income, two statistical
problems were encountered.   The Dar Es Salaam Retail
Price Index, which was used to deflate the gross domestic
product estimates, covers only those Africans who live in
Dar Es Salaam.   In 1957, only 1.5 per cent of the total population of Tanganyika lived in this city, and only 3.5 per cent
lived in towns of above 5,000 people. [15] This index, however,
is the most representative price index that is available of
African lower income groups.   In addition, it is fairly effective in indicating real production increases, e.g., the high
prices in 1961 are eliminated to show the effect of the drought
on real output (see Tables 17 and 18).

Secondly, the question arose as to whether or not the
subsistence part of production should be deflated.   The
reason that it is deflated is that it is valued at market
prices. [16] Its value, thus, is influenced directly by price
fluctuations.

One method of increasing the rate of economic growth
is through the process of capital deepening; this amounts to
the raising of the capital:labor ratio.   A rise in the capital:
labor ratio leads to an increase in labor productivity, and
consequently to a rise in the level of per capita income.   One
difficulty found in analyzing this process is the problem of
capital measurement.

In theory, gross capital formation includes two categories: (1) fixed capital, e.g., building and equipment, and
(2) working capital, e.g., stocks of raw materials, finished
goods still in inventories, and goods in the process of production.   The estimate of Tanganyika's gross capital formation, however, includes in practice only fixed capital, because
estimates of working capital are unavailable. [17] Table 19
shows the estimates of gross capital formation by type of
asset and by sector.

Estimates of capital formation created within the subsistence sector have not been attempted, excluding those
forms purchased, because of the difficulties involved in such

TABLE 19

GROSS CAPITAL FORMATION, BY TYPE OF ASSET
AND BY SECTOR, 1954-64[a]
(Ł millions)

Sector	1954	1955	1956	1957
Private				
Building and Construction	5. 4	4. 3	4. 9	5. 0
Machinery and Equipment	6. 1	9. 4	9. 1	9. 3
Total Private	11. 5	13. 7	14. 0	14. 3
Government				
Building and Construction	6. 8	7. 1	7. 4	7. 8
Machinery and Equipment	3. 4	3. 8	1. 9	2. 0
Total Government	10. 2	10. 9	9. 3	9. 8
Grand Total[c]	21. 8	24. 7	23. 3	24. 1

[a]Monetary Sector only.

[b]Because of changes in methods of measurement, these estimates are not comparable with the rest of the series.

[c]Columns may not add up to totals, because of rounding.

TABLE 19--Continued

1958	1959	1960	1961	1962	1963[b]	1964[b]
5.4	5.9	5.1	4.9	5.3	6.7	6.7
8.9	9.4	12.3	10.3	11.1	7.3	9.9
14.2	15.3	17.4	15.2	16.4	13.9	16.6
7.2	7.0	6.7	9.7	8.9	9.1	12.4
1.3	1.5	1.1	1.1	1.5	1.5	1.6
8.5	8.5	7.8	10.8	10.4	10.6	14.0
22.7	23.8	25.2	26.1	26.8	24.5	30.6

Source: The Gross Domestic Product of Tanganyika 1954-57
p. 16; Tanganyika, Statistical Abstract: 1960, p. 124;
Tanganyika, Statistical Abstract: 1962, p. 139;
Budget Survey 1963-64, p. 10; and Budget Survey
1965-66, p. 24.

measurements. These forms of capital, which are not purchased in the market, are not easily recordable as a by-
product of a market transaction. There is, in addition, a
conceptual problem in defining what constitutes capital in
this sector. Since the household is also the firm, certain
items classified as consumer goods in Western societies
have the function of capital goods in this society. For example, wives could be considered a capital asset, since
bride-price is the purchase of work rights; and because of
the wife's position, a sewing machine could be treated as a
part of the capital stock, rather than as a consumer durable.
Prest and Stewart would classify consumer durables as a
part of the capital stock. [18] Peacock and Dosser, on the
other hand, recommended excluding this group from inclu-
sion, because of the difficulty involved in distinguishing
between the consumption and capital elements in the use of
these goods. [19] This recommendation by Peacock and Dosser
was accepted by Tanganyika's government statisticians. [20]

[From the evidence, it does not appear that the Tanganyikan economy has been experiencing a quickening in the rate
of capital formation, a necessary condition to an increase in
the rate of economic growth.] From a statistical point of
view, the percentage of gross domestic product going into
capital formation is too low; and in addition, it does not
appear to be increasing (see Table 20). Simon Kuznets, in
his study, found that historically the gross capital formation:
gross domestic product ratio in rich countries is about 21
per cent; while, in poor countries, it is approximately 14 per
cent, [21] the approximate rate which it is in Tanganyika.

While the over-all rate of capital formation is relatively
low, the data indicate that the capital:labor ratio is increasing in the "capitalistic" part of the economy. Since it is generally accepted that this process is fairly slow in peasant
agriculture, [22] and the major sector of economic activity in
terms of employment is peasant agriculture; the over-all
effect of this could easily explain the low rate of capital formation for the economy.

In recent years, the industries in which labor is employed for wages have been substituting capital for labor.
African wage employment decreased from 423,167, in 1951,
to 351,801, in 1964, a decrease of about 17 per cent. The

TABLE 20

GROSS CAPITAL FORMATION AS A PER CENT OF GROSS DOMESTIC PRODUCT AT FACTOR COST, 1954-64

Year	Gross Domestic Product (£ millions)	Gross Capital Formation (£ millions)	Per Cent Column 3 ÷ Column 2
1954	141.7	21.8	15.4
1955	146.3	24.7	16.9
1956	152.4	23.3	15.3
1957	162.4	24.1	14.8
1958	167.1	22.7	13.6
1959	177.1	23.4	13.2
1960	186.2	25.2	13.5
1961	188.7	26.1	13.8
1962	203.3	26.8	13.2
1963[a]	232.3	24.5	10.6
1964[a]	244.3	30.6	12.5

[a] Data for these years are not comparable with the rest of the series, because of changes in measurement.

Source: Same as for Tables 13, 14, and 18.

major drop in wage employment occurred after 1958.[23] In
the four-year period, 1954-58, African wage employment
fell from 439,094 to 430,547, or by 2 per cent. In the three-
year period, 1958-61, wage employment fell from 430,094 to
412,092 or by 6.2 per cent. And in the three-year period,
1961-64, wage employment fell from 412,092 to 351,801, or
by 14.6 per cent.[24]

This steady fall in wage employment can be more clearly seen by examining the agricultural industry (see Table 21).
From 1953-64, wage employment steadily decreased from
212,584 to 153,410 or by 27.8 per cent.

This downward movement in wage employment has been
observed and commented upon by the government. Mr. Paul
Bomani, Minister for Economic Affairs and Development
Planning, states:

> There seems to be some relationship between average
> wages and the level of employment. It is interesting
> to observe that when average wages increased by 33
> per cent between 1962 and 1963 employment fell by
> 14 per cent and during 1964 to 1965 with an increase
> in average wages of 15 per cent employment fell by
> 5 per cent. But, during 1963 to 1964 when wages
> increased only by 7 per cent employment increased
> by 3 per cent.[25]

The evidence appears to support this statement. In the
four-year period, 1954-58, the average wage rate rose by 24
per cent, while African employment fell by 2 per cent. In
the three-year period, 1958-61, the average wage rate rose
by 55 per cent, while African employment fell by 6.2 per
cent. And in the three-year period, 1961-64, the average
wage rate rose by 83.3 per cent, while African employment
fell by 14.6 per cent.

Simultaneously with this increase in wages and decrease
in employment, there has been an expansion in the capacity of
the monetary sector, indicating a process of capital being sub-
stituted for labor. There are two indicators of this process:
(1) the yearly addition of machinery and equipment to the
capital stock, and (2) annual increases in production by wage
employers. The upward trend in the yearly addition of

TABLE 21

WAGE EMPLOYMENT IN AGRICULTURE,
1953-64

Year	African Employment
1953	225,380
1954	Not Available
1955	200,569
1956	206,411
1957	210,537
1958	212,248
1959	219,600
1960	198,616
1961	212,584
1962	192,924
1963	155,506
1964	153,410

Source: Tanganyika, Annual Labor Report 1953-61; and
         Budget Survey 1965-66, p. 27.

machinery and equipment can be seen from Table 19, while
the general expansion in terms of output of the manufacturing,
mining and quarrying, and construction industries can be
seen from Table 14.

There are at least two reasons for this apparent use of
labor-saving capital in Tanganyika: (1) wage rates have been
rising, because of the establishment of minimum wage legislation and union activity, and (2) most of the capital machinery
and equipment used is imported from developed countries,
thus forcing Tanganyika to use the relatively capital intensive
technology of these exporting nations. Julius Nyerere noted
the effects of the second reason when he cautioned African
workers not to expect to be absorbed too quickly into nonagricultural forms of employment because the plants now being built were employing the modern capital intensive methods
of developed countries. [26]

PUBLIC SECTOR

Since independence, the government's role in the process of capital formation has been greatly expanded, Tanganyika's political leaders plan to increase substantially this
role in the immediate future (see Table 22). An indication,
however, that the government has not yet appropriated the
function of the industrialist is seen by its allocation of capital
funds. The government has been channelling its funds mainly
into the creation of those forms of capital known as social
overhead capital--e.g., buildings, roads, dams, etc. (see
Table 23). As of 1964, primary responsibility for industrial
expansion had been left mainly to the private individual.

For discussion purposes, capital has been divided into
two categories--social overhead capital and industrial capital.
"Social overhead capital" includes the items in the capital
account listed under buildings and construction, while "industrial capital" includes the items listed under machinery and
equipment. Although there are many exceptions to this classification system, in that some forms of equipment are a part
of social overhead capital and some buildings are a part of
industrial capital, this type of classification approximates the
situation.

TABLE 22

GOVERNMENT CAPITAL EXPENDITURE,
1959/60-1965/66

Year	Capital Expenditure (Ł thousands)	Per Cent Change
1959/60	3,939	+ 42.5
1960/61	5,613	+ 30.8
1961/62	7,341	- 22.7
1962/63	5,674	+ 28.0
1963/64	7,263	+204.1
1964/65[a]	22,089	+ 41.2
1965/66[a]	31,184	

[a]Estimates.

Source: Budget Survey 1963-64, p. 27; and Budget Survey 1965-66, p. 37.

TABLE 23

INVESTMENT IN SOCIAL OVERHEAD
CAPITAL,[a] 1954-64

Year	Social Overhead Capital as a Per Cent of Total Gross Capital Formation in the Public Sector	Social Overhead Capital as a Per Cent of Total Gross Capital Formation in the Private Sector
1954	66. 7	47. 0
1955	65. 1	31. 4
1956	79. 6	35. 0
1957	79. 6	35. 0
1958	84. 7	38. 0
1959	86. 4	38. 6
1960	85. 9	29. 3
1961	89. 8	32. 2
1962	85. 6	32. 3
1963	85. 9	48. 2
1964	88. 6	40. 4

[a]Capital is divided into two categories: Social Overhead
Capital and Industrial Capital. The category "Social Overhead Capital" includes those terms listed under Buildings
and Construction. The category "Industrial Capital" includes those terms listed under Machinery and Equipment.

Source: See Table 18.

The effects of governmental expenditures on the rate of
economic growth have not been astounding. The rate of economic growth appears, if anything, to have fallen since the
government assumed its enlarged role in the capital formation process, i.e., the annual rate of per capita income increases was higher from 1954-62 than it was from 1960-64.
Even though the time period is too short to draw any definite
conclusions, it is interesting to speculate. Part of the explanation of this could be that the governmentally created
forms of social overhead capital have a low capital:output
ratio, even though they can be economically justified by their
long-run stimulating effects on private investment. On the
other hand, the most important reason for this lower rate of
economic growth may be simply the structural inflexibility of
the economy, thus major structural changes are needed before
a higher rate of growth can be achieved.

OBSTACLES TO ECONOMIC DEVELOPMENT

The inflexibility of the economy's structure provides a
handicap to the government's efforts to promote rapid change.
Economic life in Tanganyika is mainly dependent upon: (1)
agricultural output with a significant emphasis on production
for subsistence, and (2) world trade. The large percentage
of gross domestic product composed of agricultural output
indicates a relatively small number of attractive nonagricultural opportunities, while the large amount of economic activity put into subsistence production points out a deficiency of
high productivity employment alternatives. The strong dependence of this economy on world trade for earning money
income and acquiring capital equipment indicates the high
costs involved in implementing policies of autarky to promote
industrialization as a means of creating more productive forms
of employment.

The relative importance of agricultural production in
Tanganyika can be shown by comparing its relative size to that
of the United States. In Table 24, the various sectors of Tanganyika and the United States are grouped according to industry, in order to indicate the relative contribution of each sector to the national income of its respective country. From the
data presented in this table, it is easily observed that the output of primary goods is the dominant feature of Tanganyika's
gross domestic product, while it is the smallest component of

TABLE 24

THE RELATIVE CONTRIBUTION OF EACH SECTOR
FOR THE UNITED STATES AND
TANGANYIKA, 1964

Sector	Tanganyika		United States	
	GDP (million Ł)	Per Cent of Total	NDP (million $)	Per Cent of Total
Agriculture	140.6	57.6	17.6	3.5
Mining and Quarrying	5.9	2.4	5.7	1.1
Manufacturing	8.7	3.6	154.7	30.3
Construction	7.5	3.1	26.8	5.3
Public Utilities	11.7	4.8	31.8	6.2
Services	69.8	28.6	273.7	53.6
Total[a]	244.2	100.0	510.3	100.0

[a]Columns may not add up to totals, because of rounding.

Source: United States, Survey of Current Business: September 1965, p. 10; United States, Statistical Abstract: 1965, p. 324; and Budget Survey 1965-66, p. 4.

that of the United States. Because of this, the size of Tanganyika's gross output is rather heavily dependent upon the yearly
value of agricultural production.

There are at least two liabilities resulting from this
dependence. First, changes in the weather can greatly affect
the level of gross domestic product, e. g., the decrease in
the level of gross domestic product of 1961 has been attributed
to the drought of the same year. Secondly, sudden changes in
world market conditions can have serious repercussions on
the size of gross output, by reducing the world price of agricultural produce (see Table 25). For example, from 1954 to
1955, the price change of coffee accounted for over 87 per cent
of the decrease in the value of coffee exports; while from 1958
to 1959 a similar change accounted for over 60 per cent of the
fall. From 1956 to 1957, the fall in the world price of cotton
accounted for about 80 per cent of the decline in the value of
cotton exports, while from 1954 to 1959, the decrease in the
world price of sisal accounted for the total decline in the value
of sisal exports.

It is the plan of the government to reduce drastically the
dependence of Tanganyika on agricultural output by 1980 (see
Table 26). The attainment of a more balanced economy such
as the United States (see Table 24), is hindered, however, by
the existence of a substantial number of peasant agriculturalists
with characteristically low per-capita income and lack of skills,
and a large dependence on world trade.

The large amount of economic activity going into production for subsistence can be seen by indicating: (1) the percentage of the total agricultural land used in the cultivation of subsistence crops, (2) the percentage of the gross domestic product
composed of subsistence production, and (3) the percentage of
the income of peasant Africans earned from subsistence activities. Approximately 80 per cent of Tanganyika's land area,
and about 92 per cent of its agricultural land, is administered
by tribal authorities. Of the agricultural land administered by
tribes, estimates put the amount used in subsistence cultivation
at between two-thirds to three-fourths. [27]

Subsistence output amounts to about 30 to 40 per cent of
the gross domestic product. While this accounts for a substantial amount of economic activity, the relative importance

TABLE 25

PRICE CHANGES OF SISAL, COTTON,
AND COFFEE, 1953-62[a]

Year	Value (thousand pounds)	Quantity (thousand tons)	Average Price Per Ton (pounds)
		Sisal	
1953	12,773	171.1	75
1954	10,902	167.6	65
1955	9,956	173.7	57
1956	10,823	185.6	58
1957	9,482	181.8	52
1958	10,349	198.1	52
1959	13,057	208.8	63
1960	15,442	207.2	75
1961	14,028	200.9	70
1962	15,734	219.5	72
		Cotton	
1953	4,827	14.8	326
1954	3,357	12.1	277
1955	5,534	20.4	271
1956	7,486	27.9	268
1957	6,578	27.2	242
1958	7,249	32.1	226
1959	6,657	30.7	217
1960	8,827	38.9	227
1961	6,794	29.7	229
1962	7,393	32.6	227

TABLE 25--Continued

Year	Value (thousand pounds)	Quantity (thousand tons)	Average Price Per Ton (pounds)
		Coffee	
1953	5,809	15.2	382
1954	9,992	19.3	518
1955	6,897	18.4	375
1956	9,221	21.5	429
1957	6,960	18.0	387
1958	7,359	21.6	341
1959	5,745	19.6	293
1960	7,326	25.1	292
1961	6,762	24.6	275
1962	6,575	25.7	256

[a]Price statistics are derived by dividing the value of the output by the quantity.

Source: Tanganyika, Statistical Abstract: 1962, p. 67; and
         Tanganyika, Statistical Abstract: 1963, p. 35.

TABLE 26

STRUCTURE OF THE ECONOMY,
1964 AND 1980

	Actual 1964		Target 1980	
	Gross Domestic Product	Per Cent	Gross Domestic Product	Per Cent
Primary[a]	146. 5	60. 0	247. 8	39. 0
Secondary[b]	27. 9	11. 4	169. 7	26. 7
Tertiary[c]	69. 8	28. 6	218. 6	34. 4
Total[d]	244. 2	100. 0	636. 1	100. 0

[a]Includes: agriculture and mining and quarrying.

[b]Includes: manufacturing, construction, electricity and water, and transport.

[c]Includes: commerce, rent, and services.

[d]Columns may not add up to totals, because of rounding.

Source: Budget Survey 1965-66, p. 4; and Five-Year Plan 1964-69, vol. 1, p. 11.

of subsistence production appears to be decreasing slowly, as shown in Table 27; and, as indicated in Table 26, the government plans to hasten this decline.

The yearly level of subsistence output appears to be influenced mainly by the weather and rate of population increase. Tanganyika's statistical bureau acknowledges that estimates of subsistence production are based on increases in the farm population, with due account being given to weather conditions. The Economic Commission for Africa states in this connection: "It seems likely that subsistence production has increased at least at the same rate as the increase in population."[28] From 1954-62, the rate of increase of subsistence production, in real terms, was approximately 1.5 per cent per annum, while the rate of natural increase was about 1.6 per cent per year.

This conclusion appears to be in line with the available facts. It is generally observed that all African peasant farmers raise their own crops for subsistence, even if they are engaged in the production of crops for sale. Since the level of nonagricultural employment has not been increasing, the yearly increase in the work force[29] must then be entering almost entirely into peasant farming.

This strong dependence of peasant Africans on subsistence activity is indicated by the high percentage of total income that is composed of subsistence income, even in areas close to cash markets. The results of a Tanganyikan-village survey point this out, even though the relative dependence varies considerably with proximity to cash markets (see Table 28).

If the government attempts to industrialize the economy via restrictive trade policies, it can create an awkward situation. In order to industrialize, Tanganyika needs capital equipment. An additional factor is a ready cash market if the industrialization is to take the form of producing import-competing goods. Both of these ingredients are now supplied through the earning of foreign exchange from the sale of primary produce. Tables 29-32 indicate the extent of Tanganyika's dependence on world markets for money income and capital equipment by pointing out: (1) the type of commodities exported, (2) the percentage of gross domestic product and

TABLE 27

THE RELATIVE CHANGE IN SUBSISTENCE
OUTPUT, 1954-64
(million pounds)

Year	Gross Domestic Product (Constant Pounds)[a]	Subsistence Output (Constant Pounds)[a]	Subsistence Output as a Per Cent of Gross Domestic Product
1954	120. 5	53. 2	44. 1
1955	128. 8	57. 1	44. 3
1956	135. 7	56. 2	41. 4
1957	139. 2	59. 5	42. 7
1958	136. 5	56. 5	41. 4
1959	147. 0	58. 8	40. 0
1960	153. 3	59. 1	38. 6
1961	152. 4	59. 8	39. 2
1962	166. 0	65. 3	39. 3
1960	185. 1	62. 3	33. 7
1961	177. 2	56. 3	31. 8
1962	189. 8	61. 0	32. 1
1963	197. 5	61. 6	31. 2
1964	210. 5	64. 8	30. 8

[a]The Gross Domestic Product series from 1954-62 is deflated
by the Dar Es Salaam Price Index; the base year is 1951.
The Gross Domestic Product series from 1960-64 is given
in terms of constant 1960 pounds. The two series are not
comparable, not only because of the use of different base
years, but also because of differences in the methods used
to calculate these figures, as described earlier.

Source: Tanganyika, Statistical Abstract: 1960, p. 123;
         Statistical Abstract: 1963, pp. 146-147; and Budget
         Survey 1965-66, p. 5.

TABLE 28

CASH AND SUBSISTENCE INCOME,
1961-62

Type of Village	Cash Income	Value of Subsistence Production	Cash Income as a Per Cent of Total
	shs[a]	shs[a]	
Mountain[b]	132	1,273	9.4
Plains[b]	367	1,632	18.4
Coastal[b]	347	797	30.3
Inland[b]	210	841	20.0
Total[c]	3,918	19,432	20.5

[a]East African Shilling equals $.14.

[b]Average of villages of this type.

[c]Sum of all villages.

Source: Village Economic Surveys 1961-62, Appendix VIII.

TABLE 29

DOMESTIC EXPORTS BY MAIN ITEMS, 1954-64
(£ millions)

Commodity	1954	1955	1956	1957
Sisal	10. 9	10. 0	10. 8	9. 5
Coffee	10. 0	6. 9	9. 2	7. 1
Cotton	3. 4	5. 5	7. 5	6. 6
Hides and Skins	1. 5	1. 2	1. 2	1. 2
Oilseeds and Nuts	1. 4	1. 7	4. 1	4. 9
Diamonds	3. 1	3. 2	2. 9	3. 2
Gold	0. 9	0. 9	0. 7	0. 7
Other	5. 0	6. 8	8. 5	6. 2
Total	36. 2	36. 2	44. 9	39. 4

TABLE 29--Continued

1958	1959	1960	1961	1962	1963	1964
10.3	13.1	15.4	14.0	15.7	22.1	21.9
7.6	5.7	7.3	6.8	6.6	6.8	11.1
7.2	6.7	8.8	6.8	7.4	10.7	9.9
1.2	1.9	1.8	1.8	1.5	1.7	1.3
3.9	2.8	3.2	2.2	4.4	5.4	6.0
4.4	4.5	4.6	5.8	5.4	5.0	6.8
0.7	1.1	1.2	1.2	1.3	1.3	1.2
6.4	9.5	12.5	10.1	8.9	10.6	11.9
41.7	45.3	54.8	48.7	51.2	63.6	70.1

Source: Tanganyika, Statistical Abstract: 1956, p. 20;
Statistical Abstract: 1960, p. 30; Budget Survey
1963-64, p. 12; and Budget Survey 1965-66, p. 15.

TABLE 30

EXPORTS AS A PER CENT OF GROSS
DOMESTIC PRODUCT, 1954-64

Year	Gross Domestic Product (£ millions)	Value of Exports (£ millions)	Exports as a Per Cent of Gross Domestic Product
1954	141.7	36.2	25.5
1955	146.7	36.2	24.7
1956	152.4	44.9	29.5
1957	162.4	39.4	24.3
1958	167.1	41.7	25.0
1959	177.1	45.3	25.6
1960	186.2	54.8	29.5
1961	186.7	48.7	26.0
1962	203.3	51.2	25.2
1963[a]	232.3	63.6	27.4
1964[a]	244.3	70.1	28.7

[a]Not comparable with rest of the series.

Source: Same as Table 29.

TABLE 31

EXPORTS AS A PER CENT OF MONETARY GROSS
DOMESTIC PRODUCT, 1954-64

Year	Gross Domestic Product in Monetary Part (Ł millions)	Value of Exports (Ł millions)	Exports as a Per Cent of Gross Domestic Product in Monetary Part
1954	79. 1	36. 2	45. 8
1955	81. 8	36. 2	44. 3
1956	89. 3	44. 9	50. 3
1957	92. 9	39. 4	42. 4
1958	97. 9	41. 7	42. 6
1959	106. 2	45. 3	42. 7
1960	114. 4	54. 8	48. 0
1961	115. 4	48. 7	42. 8
1962	123. 3	51. 2	41. 5
1963[a]	156. 4	63. 6	40. 7
1964[a]	171. 7	70. 1	40. 8

[a]Not comparable with rest of series.

Source: Same as Table 29.

TABLE 32

IMPORT OF PRODUCERS' CAPITAL GOODS,
1958-62

Year	Gross Capital Formation of Machinery and Equipment (£ thousands)	Import of Machinery and Equipment (£ thousands)	Per Cent Imported
1958	10,183	8,629	84.7
1959	10,820	9,065	83.8
1960	13,372	10,881	81.4
1961	11,452	10,279	89.8
1962	12,667	9,967	78.7

Source: Tanganyika, Statistical Abstract: 1960; and Budget
Survey 1963-64.

monetary gross domestic product earned via exports, and
(3) the percentage of capital equipment imported.

In this chapter the nature and level of economic activity
in Tanganyika were discussed. Tanganyika is seen to be a
poor country with respect to its level of per capita income,
and the prospects for a rapid increase through a high rate of
capital formation are not too promising. One reason for this
state is that a large percentage of total economic activity is
allocated to agricultural output with particular emphasis on
subsistence production--an activity which is characterized by
low productivity. It was also indicated, however, that any
attempt by the government to increase the rate of economic
growth by altering the economy's structure is likely to run
into serious difficulty. For example, if the government were
to implement policies of autarky in order to industrialize,
the major source of Tanganyika's money income and capital
equipment would be cut off. In the next four chapters, the
factors contributing to the existing poor level of the economy,
as well as the obstacles to change, will be explained in greater detail.

CHAPTER 4 AGRICULTURE

The nature of Tanganyika's agricultural sector is examined in this chapter in order to point out the obstacles to using it as a growth vehicle. For discussion purposes the source of agricultural output is divided into two parts: (1) estates, and (2) peasant farms. As indicated in Chapter 3, the major portion of the African peasant's labor is allocated to squeezing out a subsistence level of living. The productivity of the peasants' farms is low because of the lack of capital and technical know-how as well as a set of tribal laws and customs which impede change. In line with the adopted ideology of the political leaders, the government has undertaken the responsibility for increasing productivity in African agriculture, by orientating production toward market sale, introducing more efficient methods of production, and increasing the capital coefficient. This chapter is divided into two sections: (1) the size and composition of agricultural output, and (2) the nature of the agricultural system--foreign enclave, peasant farms, and government programs.

THE COMPOSITION OF AGRICULTURAL OUTPUT

As indicated in Table 33, the major part of agricultural output is produced either for subsistence or for export. The indication from Table 35 is that the domestic market plays a very minor role in stimulating agricultural production. Of the agricultural output sold, the raw material group is by far the largest, and this constitutes the main part of Tanganyika's exports. The raw material group includes: (1) sisal, (2) coffee, (3) cotton lint, (4) tea, (5) tobacco, (6) pyrethrum, and (7) oil nuts. [1]

The dependence of Tanganyika's economy on the crops-- sisal, coffee, and cotton--can be seen from Table 34. Sisal is mainly an estate crop, and production has doubled from 1954-64. While Tanganyika is currently the world's largest producer, accounting for between 60.0 and 66.7 per cent of

the total African output and for about 33. 0 per cent of the
world's,[2] there has been a large increase in competition for
the world's markets in recent years. For example, Brazil
increased its sisal output by fivefold from 1953-56, and cut
drastically into Tanganyika's markets, especially that of the
United States.

Coffee and cotton are grown mainly on small peasant
farms. Productivity on these small African farms has remained low and fairly constant during the last 10 years, although physical output has increased significantly. The increase is due mainly to the output of new farms. From 1954
to 1964 coffee production increased from 23,463 to 33,200
tons, or by about 37 per cent; while cotton production rose
from 18,300 to 54,400 tons or by nearly 200 per cent.

THE ECONOMIC ORGANIZATION
OF AGRICULTURE

The economic organization of agriculture is discussed
under three headings: (1) foreign enclaves, (2) small-scale
peasant farms, and (3) government schemes.

The Foreign Enclave

A foreign enclave is defined as a pocket of production
units which use capitalistic methods of production, are operated by a foreign management, and produce crops for the export
market. These foreign enterprises exist, in many cases,
alongside of peasant farms; the native farmers, however, are
little influenced by the foreign firms, with respect to techniques of production, use of capital, and output mix.[3]

The foreign enclave consists of European estates. Almost all estate farming in Tanganyika is performed by non-
Africans on alienated land. The alienation of land refers to
the leasing, selling, or granting of land, previously considered to be in the domain of a particular tribe, to private
individuals.[4] Individual ownership or possession of land includes any association which acts as a single unit, e. g., a
corporation.

TABLE 33

CROP PRODUCTION BY MARKET SALE

| Year | Value of Agricultural Output (Ł millions) | Subsistence | |
		Value (Ł millions)	Per Cent of Total
1954	68. 3	40. 1	58. 7
1955	72. 5	42. 8	59. 0
1956	74. 4	40. 3	54. 2
1957	76. 5	43. 9	57. 4
1958	75. 1	42. 8	57. 0
1959	80. 0	43. 0	53. 8
1960	82. 5	41. 7	50. 5
1961	80. 1	43. 7	54. 6
1962	91. 8	49. 6	54. 0
1963[a]	113. 4	61. 3	54. 1
1964[a]	119. 9	56. 1	50. 1

[a]Not comparable with rest of series, because of different methods used in calculation.

[b]Residuals.

TABLE 33--Continued

Year	Export Market[c]		Domestic Market	
	Value[b] (£ millions)	Per Cent of Total	Value (£ millions)	Per Cent of Total
1954	26.4	38.7	1.8	2.6
1955	25.0	34.5	4.7	6.5
1956	31.2	41.9	2.9	3.9
1957	28.0	36.6	4.6	6.0
1958	27.9	37.2	4.4	5.8
1959	29.5	36.9	7.5	9.3
1960	37.2	45.1	3.6	4.4
1961	31.8	39.7	4.6	5.7
1962	35.1	38.2	7.1	7.8
1963	46.6	41.1	5.5	4.8
1964	50.5	45.1	5.3	4.8

[c]Assumes exports in any given year is composed of the crop grown in that year. This is not exactly the case, but the discrepancy is minor and thus the error is negligible.

Source: Tanganyika, Statistical Abstract: 1960; Statistical Abstract: 1963; Budget Survey 1965-66.

TABLE 34

VALUE OF DOMESTIC EXPORTS,
SELECTED PRODUCTS
1954-64

Year	Sisal (Ł million)	Coffee (Ł million)
1954	10.9	10.0
1955	10.0	6.9
1956	10.8	9.2
1957	9.5	7.1
1958	10.3	7.6
1959	13.1	5.7
1960	15.4	7.3
1961	14.0	6.8
1962	15.7	6.6
1963	22.1	6.8
1964	21.9	11.1

TABLE 34--Continued

Cotton (£ million)	Total (£ million)	Exports--Sisal, Coffee & Cotton as Per Cent
3.4	36.2	67.1
5.5	36.2	61.9
7.5	44.9	61.2
6.6	39.4	58.9
7.2	41.7	60.2
6.7	45.3	56.3
8.8	54.8	57.5
6.8	48.6	56.8
7.4	51.2	58.0
10.7	63.6	62.3
9.9	70.1	61.2

Source: Statistical Abstract: 1956 & 1960; and Budget Survey 1965-66.

The total amount of agricultural and pastoral land alienated as of December 31, 1960, was 3,889 square miles.[5] This amounts to approximately 5 per cent of the total agricultural and pastoral land of Tanganyika, and to about 1 per cent of its total area. Of the total area alienated, about 2,298 square miles, or 59 per cent, is agricultural land. The agricultural land amounts to 7.7 per cent of the total agricultural land of Tanganyika (see Table 35 for a breakdown of the alienated land).

The extent to which the Europeans have had an impact on the farming practices of the Africans is uncertain. Stahl states that the contribution which the Europeans have made to the economy of Tanganyika by showing the Africans proper agricultural methods of production is minimal because the Europeans engage in large-scale estate farming, while the Africans engage in small-scale peasant farming.[6] The IBRD states, on the other hand, that, "The estates. . . have a certain value in demonstrating to Africans relatively advanced methods of production. It is said that several of the more successful Chagga coffee growers have learned their methods while working as laborers on European coffee estates."[7] The IBRD, however, agrees in the main with Stahl that this impact of Europeans on the African peasant farmers has been quite small.[8]

The Europeans, on the other hand, have clearly made a large contribution to the economy of Tanganyika in the form of earning foreign exchange. The Europeans are for all practical purposes the sole growers of sisal; and in addition, this industry provided employment to about 35 per cent of the total number of workers engaged in manufacturing in 1961.[9]

The estates in the Tanga Region are mostly engaged in the production of sisal. Each of these estates is a complete unit, the labor force being African, while the management is European. The method of production used by the estates is labor intensive because of the abundant supply of cheap labor; workers are recruited from all parts of Tanganyika, Ruanda, Urundi, and the Congo.

African labor is only relatively cheap if workers are paid by the day, because of the lack of work discipline, with respect to work schedules. European employers, until

TABLE 35

ALIENATED LAND, 1960

Ownership	Total Alienated Land (square miles)	Per Cent of Total Alienated Land	Per Cent of Total Alienated Land Minus Central Government
Central Government[a]	33,438	89.15	-
Native Authorities, Cooperatives, and Marketing Boards	20	.05	.49
Semipublic Groups Tanganyika Agricultural Corporation	759	2.02	18.66
Tanganyika Packers L+D[b]	109	.29	2.68
Commonwealth Development Corporation[c]	69	.18	1.70
Mining[d]	180	.48	4.42
Private	2,931	7.81	72.05
Total	37,506	100.00	100.00

[a] This land is forest and game reserves. IBRD, p. 82.

[b] Government owns majority of the stock.

[c] After independence, this land was turned over to the Tanganyika Development Corporation. Interview, Tanganyika, Summer, 1963.

[d] Over 50 per cent of the mining lands were held under lease by African cooperatives.

Source: Tanganyika Under United Kingdom Administration, 1960, pp. 62-63; and IBRD, pp. 82-84.

recently, have paid their laborers by means of a ticket contract. Each worker has a card with thirty squares on it, and
a sticker is placed on one of the squares for each day worked.
A worker has either 36 or 42 days, depending on whether or
not housing is provided by the employer, in which to work a
minimum of thirty days. This system of payment was abolished by the government, because it felt that this system: (1)
encouraged laziness, and (2) smacked of colonialism. In its
place workers are now hired on a monthly contract so that
they must now report every day or face the possibility of dis-
missal.

Since 1952, it appears that the sisal estates have been
becoming more capital intensive. As output expands, African
employment is declining, as shown in Table 36. There are
several indicators that more capital is being used. For example, in 1959, 376 tractors were imported into Tanganyika
and the number of tractors used on estates increased from
1508 in 1958 to 1815 in 1960. [10] The mission of the IBRD
noted the use of flame guns instead of manual labor in controlling weeds. [11] The Sisal Growers Association announced
that the industry was furthering its attempt to reduce the
number of man hours per ton of sisal, because of rising labor
costs. [12]

The rise in labor costs are a result of three factors.
First, while labor is still undisciplined, with respect to work
schedules, it must now be hired and paid on a monthly basis,
rather than on a daily basis. Secondly, the legal minimum
wage has been rising. [13] And thirdly, the demands of labor
unions for higher wages and for better working conditions has
led to labor strife in the form of work stoppages.

The government has attempted to reduce the amount of
labor strife by instituting procedures for compulsory arbitration, [14] and by placing a ban on all forms of strikes. In 1961
there were 100 work stoppages, causing a loss of 113,254
man-days. In 1964 there were only forty-four work stoppages,
resulting in a loss of 61,896 man-days. [15]

The Tanganyika Plantation Workers' Union, to which the
sisal workers belong, is the largest union in Tanganyika. The
sisal section is reputed to be the most militant union in the
country. In 1958 the sisal industry lost a total of 228,908

TABLE 36

AFRICAN EMPLOYMENT IN THE SISAL
INDUSTRY, 1953-61

Year	Sisal
1953	151,800
1954	Not Available
1955	130,423
1956	133,357
1957	132,342
1958	133,803
1959	138,190
1960	121,619
1961	128,928

Source: Annual Labor Report 1954-61.

man-days through strikes. In 1961 the number of work
stoppages had been reduced, and only 45,646 days were lost.
This loss, however, accounted for over 40 per cent of the
total number of man-days lost through work stoppages.[16]

In recent years the government has been particularly
forceful in dealing with labor strife in the sisal industry.
For example, in 1962 the president of the National Union of
Tanganyika's Workers[17] and the general secretary of the
Tanganyika Plantation Workers' Union, Mr. Victor Mkello,
was deported for leading a strike of 10,000 sisal workers.
The ban on Mkello was lifted about two months later, although he was not restored to power.[18] In a 1964-65 Report,
the Sisal Growers' Association announced that the union had
finally agreed to tie wage increases with productivity increases, as a method of holding down rising labor costs.[19]

Another estate-grown crop is coffee. The amount of
alienated land used in coffee production is much smaller than
that used in sisal production. Approximately 500,000 acres
are used in sisal production, while only about 19,000 acres
are used in coffee. Unlike the White Highlands of Kenya, the
coffee estates, which are located in the Northern Region, are
not concentrated in one area but are scattered among the small
peasant farms of this region.[20]

The economic organization of these coffee estates has
traditionally been--like that of sisal--labor intensive. With
the requirement that workers must be paid on a monthly basis,
this industry--similar to the sisal industry--is tending to become more capital intensive. The average work week is
thirty-five hours for men and thirty-two hours for women and
children. Stahl notes that the working day is from 7:00 A.M.
to 12:30 P.M.[21] It is common to find the working day ending
early in this area of the world because the climate is hot and
humid, especially in mid-afternoon.

Most of the land used in coffee production is held under
a system of land tenure known as the right of occupancy. This
form of land tenure is based on individual possession; if the
land, however, is not used and developed properly, ownership
reverts back to the state.[22] Under British administration the
governor, as the sole land authority of all public lands, had
the power to grant land to individual persons. Land was

granted to native Africans as well as Europeans and Asians, with leases up to a maximum of ninety-nine years. Such grants of land were made in order to develop the agricultural potential of Tanganyika by: (1) setting an example in the use of more advanced methods of production to the peasant Africans, and (2) introducing cash crops to the area. [23]

The future of the European farmers in Tanganyika is still uncertain, but still considered hopeful as far as the immediate future is concerned. [24] As of now, the government has not instituted a policy designed to break up these estates, as is currently being done in Kenya. The government is also issuing certificates to foreign investors, guaranteeing to them compensation in their own national currency in the event that their enterprises are nationalized. [25]

There is no evidence to indicate that the owners of European estates are attempting to dump their estates on the market, out of fear of government seizure. The government has in fact indicated that it is willing to alienate more tribal land for the production of sisal by foreign companies. [26] There is evidence to indicate that this policy has met with some success. On January 1, 1964, Mr. Paul Bomani, Minister for Finance, announced that a group of French, Swiss, and British businessmen intended to invest £ 5 million in sisal cultivation. The government estimates that this amounts to an increase of 35,714 tons of sisal at the rate of £ 140 to one ton, [27] or an increase of about 17 per cent above the 1962 production level.

The government has insured, on the other hand, that the private estates will act in the best interests of the community as a whole, as defined by the political leaders. On February 13, 1962, Tanganyika's Parliament converted all land holdings held under terms of freehold to leasehold, and granted ninety-nine year leases in exchange. Rental payments and a development clause were added. The development clause specifies that the government has the right to outline the improvements which must be made to the land in order to maintain occupancy. Mr. T. S. Twea, Minister for Lands, Forestry and Wildlife, stated that this policy has been adopted strictly to encourage the development of the land to the greatest possible extent, and not for purposes of confiscation. [28] A government report on land reform states in this connection:

"Government has come to the conclusion that some land held
on rights of occupancy issued before the Land Regulations,
1948, were applied is still inadequately developed."[29]

It is difficult, in light of the government's policy toward
tribal holdings, to believe that the development of the land was
the real factor behind this policy change. The government
has not applied pressure on the Africans who hold land under
native laws and customs to convert their titles to leaseholds.
The report on Land Tenure Reform states, ". . . Broadly
speaking, title to land, under native law and custom depends
on continued occupation; if the land is not occupied, and occupation might include a long period of fallowing, the right to
the land disappears. It follows that there is, at least, some
pressure on the occupier under native law and custom to do
something with his land."[30]

This reasoning seems fallacious; for in comparing the
use of land held under freehold (estates) and under native laws
and customs (peasant holdings), with respect to efficiency, it
seems that tribal land should be the first land converted to
leasehold. The mission of the IBRD in fact recommended
just this, and listed three advantages to an individual land
tenure system: (1) peasant farmers are more secure in their
rights to the land, and thus have more incentive to invest in
their property; (2) land can be used as a security to raise
investment funds; and (3) there will be an incentive to consoli-
date land holdings.[31] It appears that the real reason probably
lies simply in the greater government control gained over the
general operation of the foreign-owned estates.

The government intends to use these foreign estates not
only as sources of foreign exchange and secondary industry,
but also as a means of promoting African participation in
sisal cultivation. The Five-Year Plan calls for the establishment of five sisal-based African settlements, with the aid of
foreign estates. These settlements will be organized on the
basis of small peasant holdings, with cooperatives having
the responsibility for marketing the produce.[32]

As part of this program, the Amboni estates, one of
the largest foreign-owned estates in Tanganyika, lent
£250,000 to the government to establish a sisal settlement in
the Tanga Region. They will also build the sisal factory and

workshops, and organize the installation of water supplies as well as supply technical assistance and develop and train supervisory staff. [33]

In addition, the government has strengthened its control over the marketing of estate crops. Mr. Paul Bomani, Minister for Finance, announced the establishment of a sisal marketing board which will have the power to regulate producers' prices. The official purpose of this board is to increase sales in new markets through a consolidated effort. Bomani, however, noted that this board would be dominated by governmentally appointed members, and would be used to increase the African's participation in sisal cultivation with the aid of financial and technical assistance provided by the Board. In 1964-65, the Sisal Growers Association allocated ₤80,000 to the advancement of Africans in sisal production.[34]

The future of these foreign-owned estates seems relatively secure as long as the political leaders believe that the Europeans are constructively contributing to the national goals. The Europeans appear willing to tolerate this partnership at least until the governmental demands reduce the attractiveness of this activity below that of other alternatives.

Small-Scale African Farms

The government placed its major emphasis in its Three-Year Plan on the development of the agricultural sector, and more particularly on raising the productivity of small-scale peasant farms. Almost 25 per cent of the expenditures of this plan were designated in this manner.[35] In the Five-Year Plan, on the other hand, the government shifted its emphasis to nonagricultural activities in order to strive after a more balanced development of the economy. Of the total planned expenditures, only 15 per cent were allocated to this activity.[36]

The government also shifted its emphasis from improving the productivity of African farms without drastically altering the existing traditional system to emphasizing the need for a complete change. In the Three-Year Plan, over 70 per cent of the expenditures on agriculture were allocated to such activities as extension work, education, and subsidization. In the Five-Year Plan, over 50 per cent of agricultural expenditures were allocated to irrigation projects and settlement schemes. [37]

The basic problem in increasing the agricultural productivity of African farms, held in accordance with native
laws and customs, appears to lie within the economic system
itself. Most observers hold the view that the tribal system
contains impediments to agricultural productivity increases
because it restricts the expression of individualism in an
attempt to preserve tribal solidarity. [38] For discussion purposes this section is divided into three subdivisions: (1) the
formalization of tribal life, (2) the effects of tribalism on the
methods of production employed by native Africans, and (3)
nomadic herders, a special problem.

The Formalization of Tribal Life

Tribalism originated as a result of a poor natural resource base and a low level of technology, and at the time
adherence to a rigid set of rules concerning production and
distribution were necessary in order for the group to survive.
These rules did not develop along standardized or uniform
lines among the tribes, but they generally emphasized the
collective good of the group. [39] Small-scale African farms are
still operated within the jurisdiction of tribal authorities and
in accord with native laws and customs, indicating that even
as economic conditions improve, there is a large amount of
inertia to change within the society.

Part of the explanation for this inertia lies in the policy
pursued by the British. Tribal authority was given legal sanc-
tion by the British shortly after World War I. [40] The British
objectives in governing Tanganyika were twofold: (1) To maintain peace and public order among the native Africans, and
(2) To work toward the eventual evolution of a modern system
of local government. [41] In order to achieve this objective the
British implemented a policy known as Indirect Rule. [42] Under
this policy, Africans were governed at the local level by native
authorities, composed of indigenous chiefs and empowered by
the British with judicial and legislative authority. [43]

From the British point of view this was a very successful political arrangement in two respects. First, it was
economical; because it minimized the number of European
officials required to govern Tanganyika. Secondly, it reduced
African opposition to potentially unpopular measures because
these measures were introduced by their own people. This

system hindered, however, the development of a nation state, and consequently an integrated modern exchange. Verma states, "The Native Administration has been criticized in some quarters on the ground that it gives a new lease of life to tribal parochialism . . . Since the Native Authority units continue to be headed by hereditary chiefs, the basic dependence on traditional loyalty still remains."[44]

From 1945 to 1961, the British attempted to fulfill the second part of their objective--to move toward a local system of modern government; but the native chiefs, who were entrenched in power, were reluctant to relinquish the formidable position which they enjoyed. By 1962 these native chiefs were still the main source of power on the local level.[45]

The Effect of Tribalism

Tribal control is highly effective when the native authority has the sole power to allocate land. In cases where the supply of land exceeds the amount demanded by households, ownership resides with the tribal authority. Members have only user rights to their individual plots. There is no incentive to change this system of land tenure to one of individual ownership, since the land's value to the individual is zero. As stated in a United Nations' report, "It was the productive effort of the individual, his wives or his servants which gave value to the land."[46] As long as he cultivates his land, his rights are secure; in addition, the individual has the right to clear and cultivate uninhabited land belonging to the tribe.[47]

This system has, at least, two negative affects on the accumulation of capital. The main method used to preserve the soil is shifting cultivation. This method involves the clearing of land, cultivating it for a specified period of time, and then moving elsewhere to repeat the same process, leaving the land to recuperate the lost fertility under bush fallow.[48] As long as land is a free factor, while labor involves a cost in terms of effort,[49] and capital is practically nonexistent, this system of land preservation is economically efficient. This system, however, is not conducive to the accumulation of capital because there is no incentive to invest in fixed forms of capital. Secondly, individualistic behavior in this society constitutes a threat to the existing political system; wealth is normally concentrated in the hands of the royal family. If an

individual were to engage openly in accumulating capital, he
is vulnerable to accusations of practicing witchcraft. [50]

For all practical purposes, there is no pure subsistence
sector left in Tanganyika. The introduction of cash crops,
however, has not automatically led to a change in the structure
of the economy to one based on individualism and specialization. The allocation function in most cases has remained in
the hands of the tribal authority: "Some lands would grow
good maize and other land only sugar cane or rice, and often
the dispersion of an individual holder over a wide area was
due to the attempt to give each member a share of each type
of soil."[51] Through this power, these authorities have imped-
ed the emergence of specialization by focusing the ties of an
individual to the tribe rather than a national market. The mission of the IBRD notes that the production of cash crops has
generally remained a subsidiary activity to subsistence production, and P. H. Gulliver states:

> By the late 1950's elements of the old economy remain-
> ed . . . Families still sought to grow as much of their
> own food as possible--doing so remained a moral as
> well as an economic ideal--cultivating more or less
> only sufficient cash crops to realize the cash income
> required to augment the family food supply and to pur-
> chase a little above the old demand for store goods. [52]

The results have been a low level of economic efficiency:

> Instead of the process (production of crops for sale)
> taking place on a stable base of an agricultural system
> planned to give an economic return, the conception of
> a cash income has led to extensive planting of land,
> particularly in maize, wattle, cotton and coffee, with-
> out any agricultural planning. [53]

Under this system, there have been little, if any, significant increases in agricultural productivity. For example, the
Sukuma are the principal producers of cotton in Tanganyika.
Land is still abundant and ownership resides with the tribe;
members can clear and cultivate any new land which they are
able to use. [54] Table 37 shows that the area under cultivation
and output have more than doubled from 1952-61, while productivity has remained approximately constant.

TABLE 37

COTTON LINT PRODUCTION

Year	Area (thousand hectares)	Production (thousand metric tons)	Yields (thousand kg. per hectare)
1952	84	14	1.7
1953	62	9	1.5
1954	101[a]	19	1.8[a]
1955	109[a]	22	2.0[a]
1956	121[a]	24	2.0[a]
1957	162	31	1.9[a]
1958	162[a]	31	1.9[a]
1959/1960	182	37	2.0[a]
1960/1961	192	34	1.8

[a]Estimates.

Source: FAO Yearbook, 1962.

A change to a land tenure system based on private
ownership appears to occur when land has a value, i.e., becomes scarce;[55] although, as mentioned, there is no guarantee
that this change will be immediate. In areas of Tanganyika
where there is no new expansion room, tribal authorities have
attempted to adjust to the new situation by reducing the size of
land holdings and the length of time land is allowed to remain
under bush fallow.[56] Both of these practices have led to a
decrease in labor productivity. The reduction in fallow time
has the same effect as decreasing the amount of the land input.

The government has turned to the use of advanced capital
equipment, e.g., tractors as a means to increase rapidly the
agricultural productivity of small African farms. The use of
this equipment has been confined to specific areas under
government supervision. The mission of the IBRD, however,
questioned the profitability of introducing this type of capital
equipment as a remedy, given the existing nature of peasant
agriculture. They list five reasons why the use of tractors is
uneconomical: (1) operating costs are too high, because of
(a) the relatively high cost of fuel, and (b) the irregular layout
of individual plots which increases the operator-hour per
acre; (2) the insufficient supply of mechanics to repair equipment; (3) the lack of spare parts; (4) the lack of managerial
skills to organize the efficient use of these tractors; and (5)
the short time for which the tractors are needed during each
year. The mission suggested that instead of introducing complex equipment, the government should concentrate on introducing relatively simple types of on-plows, wheelbarrows,
groundnut shellers, fertilizers or spraying and dusting equipment.[57]

In general it appears that a substantial increase in agricultural production cannot be gained by this tactic until the level
of technology has been raised considerably.[58] Some economists
have suggested that education is the basic means of improving
the level of technology.[59] While this may be true, it is not
enough since the basic problem is how to entice the Africans
into desiring an improved technology. This problem can be
seen from this selection of the IBRD report:

For example, it has been closely demonstrated in the
Lake Province that the yield of cotton per acre can be
at least doubled by a combination of timely planting and

weeding, tie-ridging to conserve soil and water, and the use of manure or fertilizer. The difficulty lies in promoting the adoption of such quite simple but profitable improvements.[60]

The reason commonly given to explain why the African is not highly sensitive to economic stimuli is that status in tribal society is not attained through individual economic gain. Status is based on ascription rather than achievement. This implies that the African is attached to a set of values, which excludes personal material gain. Changes in this set of values are precluded by a conservative force of tradition.[61] A substantial amount of data, however, has been found in Africa to support the hypothesis that the African is highly sensitive to rates of return.[62] The African, like his European counterpart, allocates his resources to maximize the rates of return of his factors even though he may be wary of violating tribal taboos against individualism, and is thus forced to cover his activities of accumulating wealth. Such evidence as the general use of shifting cultivation in land extensive economies is support of this hypothesis.

Since the African is sensitive to rates of return, the problem seems to lie in removing the restraints to accumulation imposed by tribal society. In the Five-Year Plan the emphasis has shifted from improving to transforming traditional agriculture through the establishment of governmentally supervised village settlements. The purpose of establishing such settlements is twofold: (1) to introduce cost reducing factors of production in order to increase the attractiveness of investing in agriculture, and (2) to overcome the conservative force of tradition by removing the Africans from tribal control.

Nomadic Herders: A Special Problem

The tribal laws and customs of nomadic herders have raised special problems with respect to the use of grazing land. The government has emphasized that the destocking of the range is a necessary prerequisite for development, because of the serious loss of soil fertility.[63] The Masai provide us with an excellent example. The Masai are nomadic herders living in an arid area of Tanganyika's Northern District. Masailand covers an area of approximately 33,000

square miles, and contains a population of about 40,000
people.[64]   The major problem of this area is the deterioration of the land.   The East Africa Royal Commission expressed its concern over the disappearance of vegetation and
water in this area, because of the lack of care given to the
land.   They state, "Laws protecting trees are never applied
and the Masai have cut and destroyed the vegetation . . .
Under current usage the region may well become a desert
within another generation."[65]

The Masai's economic system is probably the major
impediment to an improvement of this situation.   The raising
of cattle is the primary economic function of these people.
Stahl states, "The wealth and influence of a Masai rests on
his cattle";[66] while Frankel claims that animal husbandry is
more than an occupation, it is a way of life: "The tribe de-
spises all other activities than roaming with the cattle over
wide pasture areas."[67]   This attitude toward cattle is not confined to pastoral tribes.   The agricultural tribes of Tanganyika
are supposed to have this same attachment.   The Reverend
P. O. Moss described the relationship between the coffee
growing tribe, the Bahaya, and cattle in this manner: "Above
all their possessions, above kith or kin, wife or child, the
Bahaya with few exceptions love and value their cattle."[68]
J. C. Carms illustrates this point:

> Even in the stricken area there is an apathetic acceptance
> very hard for me to understand. Goats, for instance,
> are very common; hundreds of families have two or
> three. But when I ask why people do not kill them for
> food they look at me in astonishment.
>
>   'The goats are our wealth,' they say. 'If we ate
> them, what would be left?'[69]

It is commonly asserted that the African's accumulation
of cattle is not based on economic gain.   The East Africa
Royal Commission states, "Stock also provide the yardstick
of prestige and wealth, estimated unfortunately not in pounds
weight, but, like our own bank notes, in number irrespective
of condition."[70]   As a result the average weight of the cattle
is only 350 to 400 pounds.   In fact one government official
maintained that the main factor hindering the commercial
growth of the animal husbandry industry is the inability to

change the belief of the native African that his wealth and
status is based on the number of cattle owned rather than the
market values.

While it is true that the African emphasizes the size of
his herd rather than the quality, this is not evidence that this
is due to a disregard of economic gain. At the same time
that the grazing land and the water of the Masai are communally owned by different tribal clans, the herds are individually
owned, so that each individual has an interest in increasing
the size of his herd at a faster rate than his neighbor. Since
there are no restrictions on individual land use, a man will
not limit the size of his herd in order to conserve grazing
land or raise the land:cattle ratio to improve quality unless
he is ensured that his neighbor will do likewise.

The attractiveness of concentrating on quantity is further
increased by the periodic droughts which wipe out a good part
of the herd. For example in 1949, there were 1.75 million
head of cattle in the Lake area. During the drought of 1949-50
approximately one third of this herd died; but by 1953 after
several seasons of good rainfall, the herd had recovered to
its 1949 strength.

Two additional problems, besides the economic system,
which hinder the commercial growth of the industry are: (1)
lack of knowledge between prospective cattle buyers and
sellers, and (2) the spread of cattle diseases. Around the
Arusha area, the ranchers buy cattle, while their neighbors,
who inhabit an area directly south of them, normally have
cattle for sale. Neither of these groups is aware of the
other's intentions; so that while one area is overstocked, the
ranchers are going to Kenya in order to purchase cattle.

Two major proposals have been made to rectify these
problems: (1) establish a managed ranching scheme, and (2)
nationalize the cattle market. The government intends to use
exhortation and example via a governmentally managed ranching scheme to change the attitude of the Masai toward their
cattle. As noted above, the present attitude of the Masai is
not economically irrational, given their economic system. In
cases where the range is overstocked, the government has had
to rely on legal force or on taxing cattle holders according to
the number of cattle owned as a means of forcing him to part
with his cattle. [71]

The establishment of a national market will probably induce the desired effect. The government intends to market 75 per cent of the cattle sold through a cooperative system by 1970. It will be the responsibility of the cooperative to decide when to sell the cattle and when to place them on ranches for fattening.[72] The Iraqw tribe have organized markets at which cattle are auctioned off every month. At the markets of Mbulu and Dongobesh more than 5,000 people from all over Tanganyika attend each month. These markets are supervised by a government official, a livestock marketing officer, and a small African staff. There is also a market master, who is in charge of the marketing procedures, an auctioneer, and a clerical staff to record sales, etc.[73]

These organized markets bring the African cattle breeders into direct contact with prospective buyers. In this way there is an increase in knowledge, i.e., the African has a chance to test the market. White states:

> The nucleus of the gathering consists of a fairly large number of men interested in the market itself. In addition to those who bring stock for sale, there are those who attend in order to see how the prices are running. If the prices seem favorable on the first day they may decide to return home and bring one of their animals to be sold on the second day.[74]

As to the control of cattle diseases, the government is concentrating its efforts on tsetse control. Of the £210,500 allocated to disease control, £196,500 are to be spent on controlling the tsetse fly.[75]

Village Settlement Schemes

In order to promote the rapid transformation of traditional agriculture, the government is gathering African peasants into village settlements. The specific aims of this program are: (1) to raise the per capita income level of the peasants to £150 per family per year, (2) to arrest the spread of subsistence farming as a way of life and to increase the production of cash crops through the use of better farming techniques and modern forms of capital, e.g., tractors, and (3) to provide essential social services, e.g., schools, hospitals, etc. on an economic basis.[76] The third aim is necessary

because of the present location pattern of African farms. The
rural settlement scheme amounts to the movement of scattered rural hamlets into compact villages. At the present time,
it is fairly difficult to take advantage of economies of scale in
the provision of these social services.

The size of these villages will vary with the type of
farming, topography, climate, etc. The pilot schemes, however, will be limited to approximately 250 families per village,
or to about 1,000 people. To this, there must be added 15 per
cent of the population to include service personnel--tractor
drivers, teachers, mechanics, etc. [77] This scheme is based
on the implementation of block-farming techniques. This
amounts to the laying out of the fields in a pattern which will
reduce the costs of using mechanized equipment (see Figure
1). Modern agricultural equipment will be assigned to each
village, and this equipment will be used as a unit, so that the
individual peasant farmers will not handle any of this equipment.

During the Five-Year Plan, the government intends to
establish 69 of these villages. The initial capital cost is estimated at £150,000 per village plus an additional £50,000
earmarked to the training of supervisory personnel. Title to
the individual plots will be given to the peasants after the
satisfactory completion of a training program. The peasant,
however, is expected to repay his share of the costs to the
government within a twenty-five-year period. [78]

The government has also induced private individuals to
finance such schemes. One such project has been undertaken
by a private group of investors at a capital cost of £120,000.
The repayment period is estimated to be from five to ten years
at an interest rate of 6.5 per cent on the declining balance.
The repayment of this loan will be made by the individual
peasant, although the government has secured the loan.

Even if the government's plans were achieved, the
scheme's impact will probably be slight in the immediate
future. By 1970 the plan calls for a total of sixty-nine villages to be in operation with a population of about 70,000
people; the total farm population of Tanganyika amounts today
to over 9 million. In addition to this, it appears that this program has encountered recruitment problems. At the present

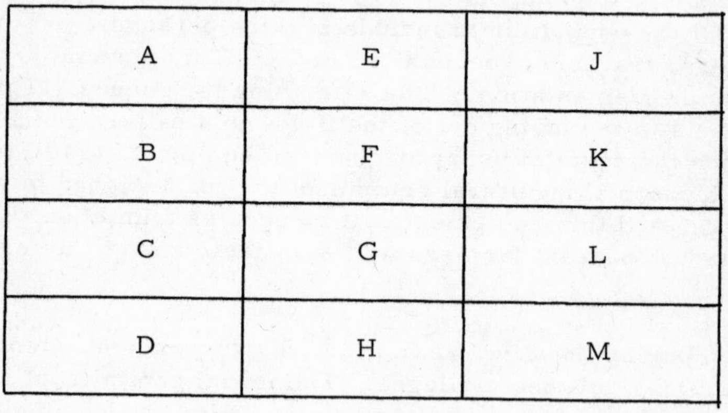

A	E	J
B	F	K
C	G	L
D	H	M

FIGURE 1.   BLOCK FARMING

Source: Memorandum No. 15, Department of Villigi-
zation, Tanganyikan Government, 1963
(unpublished Department Memorandum).

time there are approximately twenty such projects in operation with about 3,500 participating farmers and approximately
10,000 acres under cultivation. The government intends,
however, to cut back on the existing schemes and to begin no
new ones in the immediate future. The obstacle is that the
African has found it personally unprofitable to engage in this
venture. He is paid a government subsidy of 30 shillings per
month until his farm becomes profitable; in the case of tree
crops, e.g., tea, this could be up to twelve years. The opportunity cost to the farmer then is an indicator of his investment. Since sisal plantations are currently paying 150 shillings
per month, the foregone 120 shillings per month[79] discounted
during the gestation period is the cost of the investment, which
is apparently too high given the returns and discount rate.

While the high productivity area of agriculture is estate
production, major gains in agricultural productivity must come
from peasant farming, which is this nation's major economic
activity in terms of employment. Attempts to increase the
productivity of these farms through the injection of capital and
knowledge have been hindered by the influence of anti-growth
elements of tribal society. Government schemes have failed
to transform the present peasant system from one based on
subsistence to one specializing in production for the market.
From this it appears doubtful that the substantial rate of agricultural increase, projected by the planners, can be achieved.

CHAPTER **5** THE COMMERCIAL
SECTOR

Tanganyika's commercial sector is examined in this
chapter in order to point out some of the effects of government controls on the expansion of monetary activities. As
stated previously, it will be pointed out that the government
has assumed a larger role in such activities, not only to promote economic growth but also to redress a past imbalance in
the racial composition of the participants in this sector. This
chapter is divided into three parts for discussion purposes:
(1) the physical means of transportation, (2) the private commercial sector, and (3) the cooperative movement.

THE TRANSPORTATION SYSTEM

Tanganyika's transportation system is composed of
roads and railroads (there are only two navigable rivers and
these are navigable for only short distances from the coast),
and is rather limited in size. In 1962 Tanganyika had 21,459
miles of road for 45,149 motor vehicles, or about two vehicles
per mile of road. The small volume of traffic is also indicated
by the average number of vehicles using the major roads each
day, e.g., from Morogoro to Dar Es Salaam, from Moshi to
Arusha, and from Iringa to Mbeya, it was 475, 2,244, and 214
respectively in 1962.[1]

Railroad development has also been slow. The largest
rail line--The Central Line--was built by the Germans between 1907 and 1914, and stretches from Dar Es Salaam on
Tanganyika's east coast to Kigoma on the western border.
Between 1896 and 1912 the Germans also built the rail line
between Tanga and Moshi; the total route mileage of these two
lines amounts to approximately 1,000 miles. By 1962 Tanganyika's railroad system consisted of only 4,080 miles of track.[2]

Since 1958 the principal developments in railroad building have been the opening of two new railway lines: the Mnyusi-
River Link, connecting the Tanga Region directly with Dar Es

Salaam, and the Kilosa to Mkumi Line. Government officials
hope that the Kilosa to Mkumi Line is only the first link in the
plan to connect Dar Es Salaam by rail with Zambia.   This
line will open up for development the resources, especially
coal, of the Southern Highlands Region. Of the £ 11 million
allocated by the government in the Five-Year Plan to expand
Tanganyika's railway facilities, £ 6,210,000, or over 50 per
cent, is earmarked to extend this line beyond Mkumi to Kidatu.[3]

        While the size of this transport system is small, there
does not appear to be pressure for an immediate crash program to cover Tanganyika with rail lines and roads. The
volume of traffic is small as indicated, and Tanganyika's
immediate economic needs are covered.[4] Tanganyika has a
relatively insignificant cash market for agricultural produce
(see Table 33). The major areas of monetary activity, i.e.,
those areas which export raw materials and import consumer
and capital goods, are supplied with adequate transport facilities. The people in the remainder of the country are still
mostly engaged in subsistence activities, and thus have a
negligible demand for this type of service. The provision of
transport facilities to these subsistence areas would probably
stimulate monetary agricultural activity although it is doubtful
if the gain would justify the costs at the present time, given
the scarcity of capital in Tanganyika.

        Tanganyika's railroad system lies primarily in the
central and northern areas of this country. The main trunk
line runs from Dar Es Salaam in the Eastern Region to Kigoma
in the Western, practically cutting this nation into two parts.
There is one main trunk line off of this central line, which
runs from Tabora in the Western Region to Mwanza in the
Lake. The other main railroad line is the Tanga to Arusha
link, which connects Arusha and Moshi to the port city of Tanga.
In general, these railroad lines connect the major producing
areas of sisal, coffee, and cotton with port facilities. The
railroad link from Mwanza to Tabora connects the cotton industry with the port facilities at Dar Es Salaam, while the
Arusha to Tanga line connects the coffee and sisal industries
with the port facilities at Tanga.

        Tanganyika's over-all plan is to construct an integrated
transport system, i.e., to build roads which complement the
existing means rather than compete with them. The first aim

is to insure that all parts of the country are linked to transportation lines. In order to economize in the construction of
roads, the government is using as a guide a principle known
as "low-cost roads." "A low cost road is one which, having
regard to considerations of climate and traffic, has been
located and built to geometrical standards, commensurate
with future requirements, but has been constructed with bases
and surfaces to meet the present traffic requirements."[5]

The IBRD mission emphasized that the number of trunk
roads, currently existing in Tanganyika, was sufficient to
meet the needs of the nation. They recommended that the
government place its major emphasis on the construction of
feeder roads.[6] Tanganyika's political leaders, however, disagreed with this point of view and placed their major emphasis
in the Three-Year Plan on the construction of trunk roads.
This course of action was not based on promoting economic
growth, but rather on fostering political nationalism:

> The present main road system looks outward, particu-
> larly in the north and facilitates the flow of purchasing
> power from the rich provinces in the north to Kenya and
> Uganda rather than inwards to Tanganyika . . . The
> Government's view is that the new main road system
> should connect the areas of agricultural and mineral
> production (taking into consideration their future poten-
> tial) with the main outlets in Tanganyika.[7]

In the Five-Year Plan, the government announced a
change in policy to one more consistent with the recommenda-
tions of the IBRD mission. The government now intends to
give equal emphasis to the construction of trunk and feeder
roads in an effort to reach all possible developing areas,
rather than, as in the Three-Year Plan, to give three times
more emphasis to building trunk rather than feeder roads.[8]

PRIVATE TRADE

It is a commonly held view by non-Africans[9] as well as
by Africans[10] that private trade in East Africa is dominated
by the Asian segment of the population. The Asians were the
first commercial traders to penetrate this area, and are often
given credit for introducing a cash economy.[11] The future of

these people in Tanganyika is still uncertain, although there
are strong grounds for being pessimistic. The government
has attributed their monopoly position in trade to restrictive
entry practices. Mr. George Kahama, Minister for Commerce
and Industry, stated that the Asians were preventing the en-
trance of Africans into retail trade in many cases by refusing
to lease empty premises which could be used as shops. [12] Mr.
M. R. Kundya, Parliamentary Secretary to the Minister for
Commerce and Industry, stated that the Africans had been
kept successfully out of business, by a ". . . reluctance among
certain sections of the business community to advance African
participation in commerce." Kundya denounced the Asians for
showing a ". . . reluctance to put anything into the country and
little regard for the welfare of the people."[13]

        J. P. Moffett, on the other hand, while agreeing with
the government's position that the Asians dominate trade,
disagrees that the cause is the use of restrictive entry practices. He offers as an explanation the hypothesis that the
African does not take "naturally" to commerce, i. e., he
attributes the Asian's dominant position to some biological
deficiency of the African. [14] With respect to the number of
Africans who engage in some form of trade, neither of these
positions is supported by the evidence. Fergus Chalmers
Wright, in fact, challenges Moffett's opinion with the statement, "In this indigenous commerce, the distribution of consumer goods is everyman (and every woman)."[15] In 1950-52,
about 27,000 trade licenses were held by Africans out of a
total of approximately 39,000. [16] In 1961 the total number of
licenses issued was slightly more than 48,500, of which about
34,500 were held by Africans. [17] In both cases, about 70 per
cent of the trade licenses were held by Africans.

        With respect to the volume of business handled, the
Asians do hold an advantage. The African participation in the
wholesale end of trade is negligible, and the Asians handle
the major percentage of retail trade. [18] Governmental leaders
attribute the Asians' dominance of retail trade to the discrim-
inatory practices, such as charging the African retailers ex-
cessively high prices, of the Asian wholesalers, whom they
believe are cheaters.[19]

        The main evidence, upon which the government's claims
are based, is the high incidence of failures found among the

African shopkeepers.   For example, from 1950-52, the rate
of turnover was in excess of 50 per cent.[20] This high incidence of failures is more likely due to: (1) a lack of capital,
(2) a lack of managerial ability, (3) tribal attachments, e.g.,
charging lower prices to tribal members, and (4) not applying
themselves full time to this occupation.

       Very few African shops hold stock worth more than a few
hundred pounds, while in most cases the stock is worth less
than £50. Most of these shops are located in rural areas
where the size of the market is too small to attract full-time
participants to this activity. In comparison the Asian retail
shops handle a much larger volume of business. About one-
quarter of these Asian stores are located in Dar Es Salaam,
and many of these shops cater almost solely to non-African
consumers.[21]

       The tribal attachments of the Africans have also hinder-
ed their advancement in business. Africans are pressured
into charging tribal members lower prices,[22] and are expected to share their success with an ever-widening group of
relatives.[23] At the same time it is difficult for the African
to gain experience in Asian shops, because these businesses
are usually family affairs.[24] Wright did find in his study that
the few Africans who served apprenticeships in Asian shops
tended to be among the most successful African businessmen.[25]

       The political leaders plan to eliminate the prominent
position of the Asians in trade, not by promoting the growth
of a private African entrepreneurial class, but through the
establishment of a governmentally dominated cooperative
movement.[26] The choice of cooperatives as the means to
replace the Asian trader is a result of the socialistic ideology
adopted by the African leaders. The effect will be the elimination of a free market. The government's aim is to have 10
per cent by 1970, and 30 to 40 per cent by 1980, of all retail
trade in the hands of the cooperatives.[27]

                    THE COOPERATIVE MOVEMENT

       The cooperatives and statutory marketing boards are
used by the government as a means of raising development
funds and promoting an increase in the value of agricultural

produce marketed.   For discussion purposes this section is
divided into three subdivisions: (1) the nature and growth of
the cooperative movement, (2) the extent of governmental
control over its operations, and (3) the nature and governmental use of its two affiliates--the European marketing
societies and the statutory marketing boards.

The Nature and Growth

The reason for founding the cooperative movement was
to encourage and promote the production of cash crops by the
African peasants.[28]   On February 12, 1932, cooperative trading became legal, and on January 1, 1933, the first societies
were registered.   These were the Kilimanjaro Native Cooperative Union Limited (KNCU) and its eleven affiliated societies,
which were solely involved in the marketing of coffee.[29]   By
1949 there were seventy-nine registered societies, with a
total membership of 60,445 producers.   From 1950 to 1960
the growth of this movement in the area of marketing crops
has been fairly rapid as indicated in Table 38.   By 1964 the
number of cooperatives had increased to 1,200, and by 1980
the government plans to increase the number of marketing
societies to 1,600.[30]

Up to the present, the cooperative movement is mainly
composed of marketing societies (see Table 38).   In 1958
approximately Ł10 million of agricultural produce was marketed by cooperative societies; of this value, over 60 per cent
was coffee and almost 35 per cent was seed cotton.[31]   In 1960
the cooperatives handled agricultural produce valued at over
Ł13 million; this amounts to more than a third of the agricultural exports of Tanganyika, and if sisal exports are excluded,
because sisal is an estate crop, then the cooperatives accounted for over 50 per cent of Tanganyika's exports.[32]

The membership of this movement is mainly African.   In
1960 over 98 per cent of the total membership was African,
the remainder being either European or Asian.   The Asian
members belonged almost solely to the credit societies, while
the Europeans had their own marketing cooperatives.

The structure of the movement is in the form of a pyramid as shown in Figure 2.   At the bottom of this pyramid are
the primary societies, whose function is to collect the produce

TABLE 38

GROWTH OF THE COOPERATIVE MOVEMENT

Item	1950	1954	1957	1960
Registered Society	116	243	474	691
Registered Marketing Society[a]	111 (95.7)	231 (95.1)	462 (97.5)	697 (98.3)
Total Membership	81,065	196,775	300,279	326,211
African Membership	75,328	193,321	296,734	321,328
Membership of Marketing Society[a, b]	74,964 (92.5)	175,293 (89.1)	278,303 (92.7)	320,605 (98.3)
Share Capital, Reserves, and Surpluses	354,059[c]	1,145,216	2,061,494	3,269,006

[a]Percentage of total registered societies is included in parenthesis.

[b]Includes two transport societies.

[c]1949 estimate.

Source: Tanganyika Under United Kingdom Administration 1951, 1955, 1958, 1961, Part II, Appendix XIV; and The Cooperative Movement, p. 18.

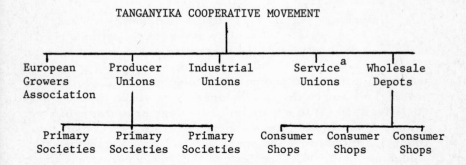

FIGURE 2.   ORGANIZATION OF THE
              COOPERATIVE MOVEMENT

[a]For example, taxicabs.

and which are composed of small-scale peasant producers of
African descent. The laws encourage the development of
primary societies along lines of race, tribe, class, or occupation. Since Africans of the same tribe are engaged in the
cultivation of similar crops, e.g., the Wachagga raise coffee
and the Sukuma produce cotton, primary societies have developed along tribal lines.

Unions are legally classified as secondary societies,
i.e., ". . . a registered society other than a primary society."[33] The functions of the marketing unions are threefold:
(1) to market, i.e., to collect, store, and sell the crops of
the producers; (2) to promote the development of cooperative
enterprises and to inspect the operations of its affiliated
societies; and (3) to engage in first-stage processing of these
crops. For example the Victoria Federation of Cooperative
Unions Limited owns and operates six modern ginneries,
valued at Ł850,000. The Bukoba Native Cooperative Union
owns a coffee-curing works, and the Kilimanjaro Native Cooperative Union is part-owner of the Tanganyika Coffee Cur-
ing Company Limited.[34] In 1964, the Victoria Federation
announced that they planned to invest Ł117,000 in sisal factories and Ł65,000 to construct a ginnery and purchase
another.[35]

The Tanganyika Cooperative Union (TCU) is the apex of
the pyramid. Its functions are to coordinate the activities
and to administer all of the cooperative societies of Tanganyika.[36] In the future the importance of TCU will be increased
as the cooperative organization is extended to other areas of
economic activity (see Figure 2).

> The first phase of the expansion of the cooperative
> movement, which might be called perhaps the
> "marketing phase," will be brought to a fitting close
> with the formation of an over-all Cooperative Union
> for Tanganyika at the end of this year. The proposed
> Union will embrace not only marketing but industrial
> cooperatives--credit and consumer societies covering
> a wide range of services and activities.[37]

One of the first priorities of the government is to establish cooperatives for the sale of consumer goods. In retail trade, the government intends to establish a chain-store

system by 1969. This system will consist of 12 small super-
markets, 250 retail shops in rural areas, and 50 mobile
shops; the total cost of this undertaking is estimated at over
₤ 1 million.   In addition, the government intends to establish wholesale cooperatives which will be able to service
about 10 per cent of the market by 1970. The government is
aiding this venture by ordering all government agencies and
all firms which have received governmental financial aid to
use this outlet in preference to private organizations. [38]

Government Controls

Tanganyika's laws give the government complete control over the operations of the cooperative societies and
unions. These powers include: (1) to prescribe the conditions under which a person can become a member of a primary society or be expelled; (2) to regulate the size of a
society; (3) to regulate the manner in which funds are raised,
loaned, and spent; (4) to specify the maximum loan that can
be made to any member and the maximum amount a society
can borrow; (5) to prescribe the conditions under which a
society can be dissolved; (6) to appoint a supervisory manager
whose duty it shall be to supervise the management of the
society's affairs; (7) to inspect and to audit the accounts of
any society at any time; (8) to provide for the appointment,
renumeration, suspension, and removal of the members of
the managing committee; (9) to bring charges against any
official of a society for misfeasance or breach of trust; and
(10) to provide for compulsory arbitration of all disputes
within a society. [39]

The government has in addition the legal power to grant
a cooperative society monopsonistic powers in the area of
marketing the agricultural produce of the peasant African. [40]
This power is being used to exclude private Asian merchants
from this activity. The government states in the Five-Year
Plan that by 1970 the marketing of African produced crops
will be handled solely by the cooperatives. All private traders, except those licensed by the cooperatives, are to be
excluded from this activity. [41]

Affiliations

There are two groups directly affiliated with the cooperative movement: (1) European producer associations,
and (2) statutory marketing boards. Tanganyika's European
agricultural producers have formed associations, some of
which are classified as cooperatives. The Tanganyika Coffee
Growers Association is a legal producers' cooperative. It
was registered as a marketing cooperative on April 10, 1945,
and has approximately 250 members.[42] The Tanganyika
Sisal Growers Association (TSGA) is not, as of yet, a legal
cooperative, but a member of the Federation of Tanganyikan
Employers. As mentioned in Chapter 4, pressure is being
applied to bring these producers under greater governmental
control, and it is highly probable that they will become a
legal cooperative in the near future.

As of now the European associations, including those
which are classified as legal cooperatives, are still essentially voluntary marketing organizations. Their chief aim is to
take advantage of economies of scale in the marketing and
processing of agricultural produce and in performing research
to lower costs of production and improve the quality of the
produce.[43] In the future it appears that an additional function
of these associations will be to promote African participation
in the production of cash crops.

The primary purpose for establishing statutory marketing boards was the same as that for establishing cooperative
societies--to encourage and to promote the production of crops
for sale by Tanganyika's peasant producers. On July 15, 1949,
the government passed the African Agricultural Products
(Control and Marketing) Law, stating as its purpose:

> When the Governor in Council is satisfied that the cul-
> tivation, production and marketing of agricultural pro-
> ducts is likely to be advanced and improved, and that
> the interests of the inhabitants of any area will be
> generally promoted thereby, it shall be lawful for him
> by order to declare that any area of the Territory shall
> be an area within which the production, cultivation and
> marketing of specified agricultural products shall be
> controlled and regulated.[44]

Tanganyika established these boards according to areas and crops, and granted them monopsonistic powers to market crops within their jurisdiction.[45] For example, the Moshi Native Coffee Board was established under G. N. Number 94 of 1952, which stated: "All Africans growing and producing coffee in the Moshi District shall comply with any directive of the Moshi Native Coffee Board as to the sale of such coffee. "[46]

The functions of the boards have varied over time. Before independence, their duties included mainly: (1) the standardizing of the quality of the export crops, (2) the levying of taxes, and (3) the stabilizing of agricultural export prices paid to peasant producers.[47] Since independence, the boards have not attempted to stabilize the prices paid to peasant producers, when it conflicts with the use of reserve funds for development purposes and have used their monopsonistic powers to exclude private traders from this activity.

The statutory marketing boards were given powers of regulation, not only over the marketing and sale of African-grown crops, but also over the production and packaging. The boards have the legal authority to:

(a) give directions as to the method of sowing, planting, cultivation, harvesting, drying, storage, processing and marketing of any specified agricultural product;

(b) order that any specified agricultural product be graded, packed or marketed in such manner as the Board may direct. [48]

The purpose for giving the boards this power is to upgrade the reputation of the quality of Tanganyika's produce. This law applies only to that produce grown on small peasant farms.[49] The IBRD mission justified the use of compulsion on grounds that many African producers were ignorant of the connection between price and quality, and that force could serve a useful function until knowledge of the workings of the market was gained. [50]

The statutory marketing boards as well as the primary societies are used by the government to collect taxes. The method of taxation is to levy a per unit cess on produce marketed.[51] In addition, the boards are legally permitted to collect revenue for a reserve fund. The functions for which these funds can be used are specified in the law:

> (a) payment of the expenses of charges by the Board and for which the Board may become liable in the course of its duties;

> (b) payment of such staff as the Board may have employed in carrying out its functions;

> (c) the marketing and advertising of any specified agricultural product;

> (d) the provision of such services as the Board considers necessary to promote the economic development, production or preparation of any specified product, or to assist the producer in carrying out the provisions of the Ordinance or the provisions of any other law for the time being in force relating to the cultivation, preparation, handling, or marketing of any specified product or the prevention or eradication of the diseases thereof;

> (e) such other purposes as may be prescribed.[52]

In order to promote the growth of cash cropping, as specified in Section 14 (1) d, the government planned to use the reserve fund to stabilize the agricultural prices paid to peasant producers.[53] Stabilization is defined as a reduction in the amount of fluctuation in prices paid to or income received by peasant producers from year to year. Tanganyika's statutory marketing boards have attempted from time to time to stabilize the prices paid to the native African farmers. The results have been poor because of a lack of funds for this purpose. For example, in 1962, the Cashew Board successfully stabilized the prices paid to farmers, as the world price fell; the board, however, was forced to discontinue this operation after three months because of a shortage of funds. In 1966 a Presidential Commission recommended the permanent discontinuation of these schemes because of their invariable failure to accomplish their purpose.[54]

The main benefit to development gained from stabilization is the protection of peasant primary producers from experiencing sharp losses in income caused by a sudden fall in
world prices. P. T. Bauer states:

> The case of paternalism can be regarded as an educa-
> tive restraint to apply Professor Hutt's vivid phrase.
> The sharp and discontinuous fluctuations in the prices
> and output of primary commodities often affect producers
> who have only comparatively recently joined the money
> economy, and although there is much evidence of their
> ability to take the long view, they cannot be generally
> expected to envisage the temporary nature of their pros-
> perity and to set aside part of their proceeds in good
> times. [55]

The economic benefit then is a reduction in the risk factor
involved in the production of cash crops. If peasant producers
did not hedge against sudden price declines, the result of a
fall in income to producers close to the margin of subsistence
could be starvation conditions, and consequently a disillusion-
ment with producing for exchange. At the present time, Tanganyika's peasant producers hedge against this risk by producing their own subsistence crops;[56] the problem is to
increase their attachment to the market.

The reduction of this risk by operating stabilization
schemes is not costless. These schemes are based on the
assumption that small-scale producers must be protected
and insulated from the forces of a free market. In doing
this, the contact of these producers with new ideas and wants
is also reduced; and it is made, consequently, more difficult
to change the parochial nature of tribalism. [57]

The East Africa Royal Commission claims that the
basic problem in promoting the production of cash crops is
the lack of motivation or incentive to work for cash on the
part of the Africans. [58] President Nyerere, however, believed
that this could be accomplished without relying on the free
interaction between African peasants and the market. He
planned to rely on education, exhortation, and example. [59]
The East Africa Royal Commission criticized this attitude on
the following grounds:

We have been impressed by the fact that over a period
of years government policy has appeared to accept the
view that this alleged conflict does in fact exist (between producers and private traders) and that it must
be dealt with by the creation of state-regulated producer
monopolies, and by state regulation of whatever trading
functions it is thought convenient to leave to the ordinary marketing system. In our opinion, this view is
founded on a misapprehension of the function of the
ordinary marketing system. In particular it fails to
recognize the mutual dependence of producers and consumers which is effected through the price mechanism
of the market and by the activities of specialized traders in developing new consumer wants and new markets
for producers. It is fallacious to assume that the commercial system of distribution is merely an appendage
to the process of production. It is part of the productive process itself. The market is not static but a
dynamic part of the economy and its growth is as vital
to the producers of primary commodities as it is to all
other producers and consumers. We have already made
clear that it was the opening-up of new markets which
alone made possible an escape from tribal subsistence
economy in the past. Similarly the widening of markets
can alone bring about an expansion of the economy in
the future. To frustrate the extension of markets is to
restrict the expansion of the economy. [60]

As throughout Africa, the main reason that this system
has not been used successfully to stabilize producers' incomes is that it has proved to be an excellent way to divert
funds from the peasants to national development schemes.
For example, in 1954, the Cotton Seed and Lint Board announced that £ 2. 5 million had been lent to the government
from their Price Assistance Fund for investment in long term
development projects. [61] In 1960 the Cotton Marketing Board
lent their societies £ 162, 683 for the purchase of capital
equipment. [62] In 1964 Mr. J. S. Kasambala, Minister for
Cooperative and Community Development, stated that the
cooperatives had an annual surplus of between £ 2. 5 million
and £ 3 million which could be invested rather than redistrib-
uted to native producers. [63] What Kasambala fails to mention,
however, is that this surplus is accumulated each year only
as a result of the marketing arrangement.

The statutory marketing boards estimate the world price for the coming year. This price is set after the crop is planted, but it is subject to change at any time during the year. The price, established by the Board, is based on an estimate of world market conditions, although the average price of the preceding year is usually used. The primary societies, which are directly responsible for the collection of the produce from the native producers, advance up to 75 per cent of the estimated value of the crops, less the expenses of marketing and an excise tax, to the producer. By law 75 per cent is the maximum amount that can be advanced on the security of crops, [64] and in practice this is the amount that is usually advanced. The remaining 25 per cent is then held in a reserve against the possibility of a fall in the world price. If the estimate proves to be accurate, the remaining 25 per cent is refunded to the producer minus a tax by the government and a cess by the board for the reserve fund. This deduction usually amounts to about one-half of the 25 per cent, and the remainder constitutes Kasambala's surplus.

Besides insulation from market forces, the use of this marketing arrangement has imposed additional obstacles on increasing monetary agricultural output. First the method of diverting funds amounts to a direct tax on the incomes of peasant producers and acts to discourage the production of, and thus investment in, crops for sale. The burden of these taxes falls completely on the African producer because the world demand for African produced crops is perfectly elastic, [65] while the supply curve is rising because of the opportunity costs involved. [66] One likely effect of this type of taxation is an increase in the production of subsistence crops because in effect this method of acquiring funds acts as a subsidy to this activity plus the migration to wage employment. The likely effect on investment, if subsistence activity plus migration becomes more attractive, is a reduction in the purchase of such modern forms of capital as insecticides, ploughs, fertilizers, etc.

A second burden stems from the government's efforts to internalize the entire marketing system by substituting the directives of cooperative officials for the direct signals of the market. The basic problem is the lack of an adequate supply of properly trained decision-making personnel. The policy to insure maximum efficiency in trade under these conditions should be to increase reliance on the market

mechanism rather than decrease it. It appears that the
elimination of the private trader and the establishment of a
centralized trading organization has resulted in the internali-
zation of diseconomies rather than economies. The Presidential Commission on Cooperatives emphasized the problems
which developed from the lack of a trained and honest staff.
Farmers charged that they were normally victimized by in-
competent and corrupt officials, and the Commission reported
that the farmers were invariably shortchanged through the use
of faulty weights, etc. It appears that the cooperative movement has not been an adequate measure either to protect the
poor African farmers from the guile of alien traders or to
facilitate the marketing of crops, and thereby increase the
attractiveness of this activity. [67]

     In conclusion, the government has attempted to promote
cash activities by peasant Africans by substituting a cooperative form of trading for a free enterprise system. The decision to use cooperatives is based on the acceptance by the
political leaders of the ideology known as African socialism,
which is in turn based, at least in part, on the domination of
trade by an alien group. The success of the cooperative
movement, with respect to increasing the attractiveness of
cash activities to the African peasant by improving the efficiency of the trading system, seems doubtful. The fact that
cash cropping is heavily taxed via the cooperative system
relative to subsistence production creates uncertainty as to
what the real purpose of this scheme really is. It would
appear from Tanganyika's experience that nations which have
a shortage of decision-making talent and a problem of eliminating restrictive tribal institutions would be wise to increase
reliance on a free market system rather than decrease it.

CHAPTER 6   THE MANUFACTURING SECTOR

In Chapter 1 it was indicated that Tanganyika lacked such basic mineral resources as coal and iron, while in Chapters 4 and 5 it was pointed out that the economy was characterized by a low level of per capita income with a large portion of the population underemployed in agricultural activity. The purpose of this chapter is to examine Tanganyika's manufacturing sector with respect to its growth potential. The aim of the political leaders is to increase the relative contribution of this sector in order to redress the present imbalance of the economy. This chapter is divided into three sections for discussion purposes: (1) the obstacles to rapid industrialization, (2) the present structure of manufacturing activity, and (3) the government's program of industrialization.

OBSTACLES TO THE PROCESS OF INDUSTRIALIZATION

Tanganyika has six major obstacles to the development of secondary industry: (1) the lack of certain basic mineral resources, (2) the small supply of electric power, (3) the shortage of skilled and disciplined labor, (4) the small size of the internal market, (5) the shortage of industrial-managerial skills, and (6) the backwash effects caused by the creation of the common market among Tanganyika, Uganda, and Kenya.

The Lack of Certain Basic Mineral Resources

In Chapter 1 it was pointed out that Tanganyika is not producing in any significant amounts certain mineral resources which are necessary for the growth of basic industries, e.g., coal, iron, and oil. The minerals which they do produce are exported, for all practical purposes, in their natural state. Diamonds and gold account for the major percentage

of Tanganyika's mineral production; and while these do supply
foreign exchange, their production does not facilitate the
growth of such basic industries as steel or lead to secondary
processing activities.

The Small Supply of Electric Power

Tanganyika's total supply of generated electric power
is small but concentrated into those areas of greatest demand.
In recent years, the rate of growth has been relatively high
as shown in Table 39, e.g., from 1950-62 it increased by 270
per cent. The major sources of the increased demand are
industrial and commercial firms and household units in urban
areas (see Table 40).

Since 1953 the major growth in power output has been
supplied by thermal plants because of the lack of permanent
rivers with which to generate hydroelectric power (see Table
41). The problem with using thermally, rather than hydro-
electrically, produced power is the higher costs resulting from
the use of imported fuel. [1] With a serious shortage of investment funds acting as a constraint, the IBRD mission recommended, and the government concurred, that effort should be
concentrated in developing the power capacity in the Eastern,
Northern, and Tanga Regions because: (1) these regions are
well-supplied with permanent rivers, and (2) these areas are
the major sources of economic activity. [2]

In the Three-Year and Five-Year Plans, estimated
governmental expenditures were Ŀ1.8 million and Ŀ8.1 million, respectively, with the people of the Eastern, Tanga, and
Northern Regions being the main beneficiaries. The Hale
Hydroelectric Project is the government's highest priority
scheme. Its purpose is to supply cheap power to the people
of this area by harnessing the waters of the Pagani River at
a cost of about Ŀ10 million. [3] It is estimated that this scheme
will save 3.2 cents per kilowatt over power supplied by thermal plants.

Besides the limitation of investment funds, the major
drawback to an expansion of Tanganyika's capacity is not the
shortage of technical ability, but a lack of sufficient effective
demand to warrant economically a large power program. The
major obstacle is the small number of industries and urban

TABLE 39

GENERATED POWER, 1950-61

Year	Generated Power (millions of KWH)
1950	48.6
1953	88.1
1954	100.4
1955	111.9
1956	124.1
1957	131.9
1958	141.2
1959	145.9
1960	154.8
1961	164.3
1962	179.2

Source: Tanganyika, Statistical Abstract: 1962 and 1963.

TABLE 40

POWER SALES
(thousands KWH)

Year	Domestic Supplies	Industrial and Commercial Power
1953	16, 787	34, 405
1954	18, 164	43, 648
1955	20, 496	40, 091
1956	23, 142	54, 076
1957	26, 248	57, 773
1958	27, 288	64, 309
1959	30, 005	69, 200
1960	32, 554	74, 618
1961	34, 004	81, 053
1962	36, 814	91, 982

Source: Tanganyika, Statistical Abstract: 1962 and 1963.

TABLE 41

GENERATING CAPACITY OF POWER

| Year | Nature of Plant | |
	Diesel (KW)	Hydraulic (KW)
1953	11,492	19,200
1954	13,716	19,200
1955	15,292	19,080
1956	17,733	19,080
1957	19,512	19,080
1958	19,852	20,080
1959	22,352	20,200
1960	20,161	20,200
1961	26,347	20,200
1962	28,383	20,200

Source: Tanganyika, Statistical Abstract: 1962 and 1963.

areas. Tanganyika's population, as indicated in Chapter 2,
is widely dispersed throughout the country in small scattered
hamlets, and as a result, it is difficult to service economically the far majority of the people. At the present time,
about 80 per cent of Tanganyika's consumers of power live in
the fourteen towns of 5,000 people and over.[4]

The government has no plans for instituting a crash
program to construct power plants all over the country in an
effort to stimulate economic activity. It cannot be guaranteed
that the availability of power will automatically elicit a demand.
Since the opportunity cost of development funds is high, the
wise policy seems to be the present one--to supply power mainly to those areas which already have a sufficient level of demand to warrant the outlay of funds, and which can be supplied
relatively cheaply with hydroelectric power.

The Shortage of Skilled and Disciplined Labor

Tanganyika's basic labor problem is the low productivity
of the African wage-earner. This is evidenced by the low
wage rates received by them. In 1962, the average compensation of African workers was less than 100 East African shillings
per month ($14). The lowest paid area of private activity in
1962 was agriculture, where the average wage was 80 shillings
per month ($11.20), although these workers were supplied in
addition with a food and housing allowance.[5]

The East Africa Royal Commission pointed out the
dilemma of the government with respect to raising wage rates:
"Much of the evidence which we received emphasized the
mutual relationship between low wages and low labour productivity; wages were low because the labour was inefficient and
the labour was inefficient because the wages were low."[6] The
two major labor obstacles to productivity increases through
the creation of nonagricultural forms of employment, e.g.,
manufacturing, are: (1) the lack of skills, and (2) the lack of
factory discipline. In 1962, of the 387,670 Africans engaged
in wage employment, 198,941 were in agriculture, or slightly
over 50 per cent. Most of these are unskilled laborers. In
all, there are less than 100,000 laborers in Tanganyika who
could be classified as skilled, i.e., bricklayers, carpenters,
clerks, etc.[7]

One basic problem which contributes to the inefficiency of African workers is the lack of industrial discipline. Stahl states that the European estates employ approximately one-third more workers than needed because of the high rate of absenteeism.[8] Difficulty has also been encountered in hiring 1,000 laborers, disciplined with respect to industrial life, to perform routine tasks in a cashew plant. J. E. Goldthorpe attempted to explain this situation in the following manner: "Fresh from the country, . . . men are unused to the regular hours of factory work, and irregular attendance, utter incomprehension, and childish irresponsibility together with low output and inefficiency, make the services of African labourers of little economic value."[9] The Arthur D. Little Report summarized the problem in a similar manner: "For want of industrial experience, labor is generally unskilled and unaccustomed to the disciplines (regular and prompt attendance, quality standards, etc.) necessary to efficient industrial production."[10]

The solution to the first of these problems--lack of skills--involves a dilemma. Industrial skills will only be sought by the Africans if manufacturing concerns are already established and demand these skills as a condition of employment. The East African Royal Commission states: "Labour is not normally trained in vacuo . . . ."[11] At the present time, manufacturing firms desiring labor with a particular skill have to train these workers themselves because of the shortage of educational facilities of this type. The normal training period is about three months for fairly routine jobs. The over-all effect is that labor is not cheap after the costs of training are added.

Some have suggested that the small supply of skilled labor is partly due to the closed shop operated by the Asians. The East Africa Royal Commission states, "It was represented to us, too, that many of the skilled crafts in industry were practiced by Asians who, while not openly pursuing a policy of racial closed shop, offered powerful resistance to any form of African participation."[12] Little evidence was found to support this charge. Whatever the reasons, the short supply of skilled labor does act as a major obstacle to the expansion of manufacturing activity by reducing the expected rate of profits.

The second problem--lack of discipline--contributes
to the low productivity of labor by reducing its efficiency.
This problem is more difficult to solve than the other because
it involves a basic change in the economy's structure, such
as permanent attachment to paid employment in urban areas
and the end of migration back to rural homes. [13] For example,
there are many African males who leave their families and go
to work in the city during the nonagricultural seasons. These
people leave the city, however, without notice to their employers and return to their lands during the planting and
harvesting seasons. [14] There is thus little incentive to learn
skills and form new habits, which are a prerequisite for the
efficient use of labor.

In order to reduce the amount of internal migration,
the government passed a minimum wage law and abolished the
ticket contract. [15] Because many of the marginal firms
would be forced out of business, the Report on Minimum
Wages recommended that caution be exercised in setting a
minimum wage in agriculture. No such restraint was exercised in dealing with urban European employers. In 1962,
the minimum wage of house-servants was raised to 150
shillings per month. Unemployment was the immediate
result; within forty-eight hours after the minimum wage went
into effect, 800 house servants reported that they had been
dismissed. [16] In most cases, this unemployment was a
result of the Europeans reducing the number of domestics
which they employed. In general, the effects of minimum
wage legislation has been an increase in unemployment,
which has led to unrest in the city. At Nakuru, 1,500 unemployed workers threw stones at the Labour Exchange after
being told there were no jobs available. Mr. Baghdelieh,
Parliamentary Secretary to the Minister for Labour, told
workers in the cities throughout Tanganyika to return to the
land if they were unemployed. [17]

Tanganyika's over-all unemployment problem, however,
is minor because of the relative unimportance of wage-employ-
ment, i.e., the primary labor problem is under-employment.
The East Africa Royal Commission states: "Taking the East
African economy as a whole there is no evidence of unemployment as that is commonly understood. "[18] The term under-
employment means disguised or concealed unemployment, [19]
or low productivity. The East Africa Royal Commission states:

"There is also evidence of concealed unemployment or under-
employment in the congested areas and elsewhere. The
extent of actual unemployment and under-employment cannot
be measured on the basis of the available data but there is
general agreement that it is considerable."[20]

If underemployment is the major labor problem, the
question arises as to what significant effect minimum wages
can have on Tanganyika's wage structure. The major problem is a lack of high earning opportunities in nonagricultural
forms of employment. It appears that effort should be
directed toward creating such alternatives rather than
thwarting its growth through higher labor costs. The government has admitted that minimum wage legislation has led to
the more economical use of labor, and now has implemented
a new labor policy of linking wage increases to productivity
increases.[21]

The Arthur D. Little Report advocated that labor
unions be used to lower labor costs by increasing the African's
industrial discipline.[22] The government has agreed, and the
present role of Tanganyika's unions is to enforce industrial
discipline and to help these workers adjust to urban and
industrial life.[23] Mr. J. O. Mbaga, Assistant Secretary
General of the National Union of Tanganyika's Workers,
stated that the primary purpose of unionism is to help build
the country and to improve the living standards of the workers
through industrial growth.[24] This does not mean that the
unions are to become mere instruments by which employers
can control their workers. The government states in fact:

In an independent socialist state, where the aims of
the government and workers are the same, employers
should change their conservative attitude towards the
workers. Capital and labour depends upon each other,
and therefore management and workers should closely
cooperate on matters which affect the industry. Labour
relations should reflect the political ideology of the
country where the dignity of the workers is fully recognized. The rise of labour as mere tools for production
should cease by requiring employers to justify their
industrial decisions to the Workers' Committees before
taking action.[25]

While the political leaders intend to reduce industrial strife
and to restrain labor's demands for higher wages through
their domination of the unions, they plan at the same time
however to limit the employers' powers by infringing on what
is normally considered to be management's prerogatives.

The government has the legal power to designate which
unions are to represent a particular group of workers, and has
banned all strikes and lockouts. [26] Unions and employers bar-
gain collectively to determine wages, hours, and conditions.
If an agreement cannot be reached, then the matter is referred
to the Labor Commissioner, who appoints a conciliator. If
this procedure is unsuccessful, the Labor Commissioner can
appoint an arbitrator, if both parties agree. If one of the
parties does not agree to arbitration, then the Minister for
Labor establishes a board of inquiry to examine the reasons
why this party refuses to arbitrate voluntarily. During the
time of inquiry (fourteen days), there can be no strikes. If a
report is not forthcoming in fourteen days, then the union
could strike, although it has never happened. If after the
report is submitted, the minister decides that the dispute is
to be settled by compulsory arbitration (which is the normal
procedure), then an arbitrator is appointed by the minister.
The decision of the arbitrator is binding; although it can be
appealed to the minister, the decisions have never been
reversed.

In February, 1964, the trade unions were made an arm
of the government. The name of the national union was changed
from the Tanganyika Federation of Labor to the National Union
of Tanganyika's Workers, and the Labor Ministry was integrated with the trade union movement. Mr. Kamaliza, Minister
for Labor, became the first general secretary of this new
union. [27] The reasons for bringing the trade union movement
directly under the control of the government was not only to
increase the government's effectiveness in attracting foreign
investment by maintaining stability and peace, but also to gain
control of the union's funds. Kamaliza rebuked some of the
union's leaders for demanding the nationalization of industries.
He told these leaders that Tanganyika was relying upon foreign
investment to raise the standard of living. [28] In February,
1964, Kamaliza stated that the role of the unions was to assist
the government ". . . in implementing effectively its socialistic policies. "[29]

As to the funds, the government desired to use the union treasury for development purposes. Kamaliza complained that the Plantation Union had spent Ł71,650 of the Ł74,950 collected, or 95 per cent, for administrative purposes. He stated that since Tanganyika had a serious shortage of capital, caution should be exercised in the expenditure of such funds. The union must now submit to him all estimates of expenditure for approval. As a guide, the union is allowed to spend up to 40 per cent of its revenue on administration.[30]

The government has attempted to smooth over this usurping of control by granting to the workers certain concessions. Just prior (January, 1964) to the formation of the union, the government passed a law establishing a social security system.[31] In March, 1964, the government announced that the union was going to build low cost housing for the workers. In return Kamaliza asked that labor work hard, back the government, and be patient.[32] In May, 1964, the government ended the right of private firms to dismiss their workers arbitrarily before consulting with the union.[33]

In October, 1963, when this merger was first proposed, Mr. Tandau, then general secretary of the Tanganyika Federation of Labor, opposed it on grounds that it ended free trade unionism in Tanganyika. In February, 1964, Mr. Mtaki, Minister of Parliament, stated the government's position: "Tanganyika should be a country with one party, one union, and one newspaper."[34] In May, 1964, Kamaliza justified the government's position with these words: "It was useless for Africa to copy foreign concepts regardless of whether they would help to improve the standards of the people."[35]

The prohibition of a free trade union movement is defendable if industrialization is Tanganyika's primary goal. Such governmental control is necessary in order to prevent a sharp increase in wages and in industrial strife. A rise in labor costs would have two adverse effects on industrialization plans: (1) it would lower the expected rate of profits of investment opportunities, and thus eliminate those which are marginal, and (2) it would decrease the amount of savings available for investment.

The Small Size of the Internal Market

The size of Tanganyika's market for manufactured
commodities acts as an obstacle to the growth of industrial
production. In Chapter 3, the people's low level of income
was indicated; while in Chapter 4, the large amount of economic activity devoted to subsistence production was discussed. Arthur D. Little summarized the situation:

> The economic life of Tanganyika is based primarily
> upon small-scale peasant farming and animal husbandry.
> The self-sufficiency of individuals and family groups is
> suggested by the very small number of employees with-
> in the country. [36] . . . Present internal markets for
> most products are small (in many instances far below
> economic plant size) and there is great uncertainty as
> to which products consumers will wish to buy first, as
> their cash incomes increase with a general develop-
> ment of the economy. . . . [37]

The Lack of Entrepreneurial Skill
in Manufacturing

Another serious handicap to the process of industrialization is the lack of entrepreneurial activity in secondary
industry. As discussed in Chapter 5, entrepreneurial activity has been confined to the Asian segment of the population.
These people, however, have restricted their efforts to trade.
As for the African's entrepreneurial activity, the Arthur D.
Little Report noted that there has been no significant development of this skill up to the present time. [38]

The Common Market

Tanganyika has entered into a common market arrangement with Kenya and Uganda. This arrangement covers such
activities as: (a) a common service organization to operate
the railroads and the airlines in these countries, (b) the
maintenance of harbors and the collection of duties at these
ports of entry, and (c) the free flow of goods and the unrestricted movement of all factors of production among these
nations.

This common market will most likely be a positive
force in aiding the industrialization of East Africa as a whole
by widening the size of the internal market. [39] Tanganyika's
political leaders, on the other hand, fear that potential investors, both foreign and domestic, will be attracted to the
Nairobi area in Kenya in preference to possible sites in Tanganyika, because Nairobi contains major inducements to new
enterprises. [40]

Concentrated in three areas of East Africa is the major
wealth and purchasing power: (1) the Kenya Highlands, (2)
the Victoria Basin, and (3) the Moshi-Arusha area. East
Africa's railroad system stretches west and south from
Nairobi, connecting these three areas with Nairobi as the
nucleus. Nairobi also has the advantage of being the first and
largest commercial center in East Africa, containing the home
office of most of the commercial and industrial firms as well
as the East Africa Common Service Organization. Besides,
it has the largest supply of social overhead capital. The city
contains: (1) the best water supply, (2) industrial sites, (3)
good communications--roads and telephones, (4) proximity and
direct link by rail to the largest seaport in East Africa--
Mombasa, and (5) the largest pool of skilled labor.

The more rapid industrial growth of Kenya has led Tanganyika's political leaders to seek concessions from its partners in redressing this situation. The Kampala agreement of
1964 granted to Tanganyika the exclusive right to produce
certain items, as well as to impose temporary quotas and to
offer greater incentives to new firms. [41] Whether these concessions are adequate to overcome the natural advantages of
Nairobi remains to be seen. Given the present strain on relations between the three countries imposed by Tanganyika's
nationalization of certain enterprises, it appears very likely
that Tanganyika's leaders will withdraw from the common
market in order to increase their own industrialization process.

The Manufacturing Sector

Manufacturing activity includes mainly: (1) the processing of agricultural commodities for sale in the export market,
and (2) the manufacture of import-competing goods for sale
in the domestic market. Up until recently, the rate of

expansion of import-competing goods has been very slow
because of the small size of the internal market. The IBRD
mission states: "There are obviously many manufactured
items which it would be difficult or impossible to displace by
domestic production, either because the technical conditions
for their production do not exist or because the local market
is still too small to permit production on a profitable basis,
even with substantial protection against imports."[42] The
expansion of both types of manufacturing activity is mainly
dependent upon the expansion of agricultural commodities.
This is due to: (1) processing activities being dependent upon the supply of agricultural products; and (2) demand being
dependent upon rising incomes, and rising incomes being
dependent upon the expansion of agricultural activities.

There are nine existing classifications of manufacturing: (1) primary processing, (2) secondary processing, (3)
goods manufacture, (4) building materials manufacture, (5)
assembly, (6) repair and maintenance, (7) service, (8) basic
utilities, and (9) others.[43] Table 42 shows examples of each
of these classifications.

Primary processing is Tanganyika's largest manufacturing division. In 1961, the total work force of manufacturing
establishments was over 80,000. Of this, about 45,000, or
over 50 per cent, were engaged in primary processing.[44] In
the same year, this activity's contribution to net output was 46
per cent, while the wage bill of primary processing amounted
to over 52 per cent of the total payment to labor in manufacturing.[45] As for the manufacture of import-competing goods,
this activity only amounted to 20 per cent of manufacturing's
total net output, while the wage bill and the number employed
accounted for about 20 and 25 per cent, respectively, of the
totals.

The major employer of labor is sisal processing. In
1962, about 27,000 people, or over 60 per cent of the total
work force employed in primary processing industries, were
involved in sisal and sansevieria processing.[46] Since sisal
is an estate crop, this is an indicator of the large contribution that the Europeans have made to the development of Tanganyika.

In the Five-Year Plan major emphasis has been given
to the expansion of manufacturing activity designed to service
East Africa's internal market. By 1970 this activity is expected to contribute twice as much to manufacturing's total
net output as primary processing.[47] This involves a complete reversal in the present structure of Tanganyika's manufacturing sector.

GOVERNMENTAL PROMOTION OF
PRIVATE INDUSTRY

The government has established an Industrial Studies
and Development Centre in order to promote the expansion
of manufacturing activity. The duties of this Centre involve
basically assisting in the establishment of new firms, as well
as recruiting new ones. The forms of assistance offered
are: (1) tax reductions, (2) market and industrial research,
e.g., measuring the internal demand for particular products,
(3) small loans to native Africans to establish small-scale
manufacturing firms, e.g., household utensils, and (4) promoting the sale abroad of Tanganyika's products through
trade fairs, etc.

The policy of the government is to grant generous tax
reductions to new corporations. The depreciation allowance
on industrial plants and equipment is an initial 20 per cent
and the remainder deducted on straight time over a six year
period. Tax concessions are also given on import duties.
The government refunds duties paid on raw materials imported for industrial use. There are two requirements for
an investor to be granted this concession: (1) the raw materials must not be available on the domestic market, and (2)
the benefits to the country from this activity must exceed
the duty revenue lost. Estimates of the total benefit to the
country from an industrial enterprise are based on the following criteria: (1) gains in income tax receipts, (2) increase
in employment, and (3) the stimulation of further manufacturing activity.

Tanganyika's Ministry for Industry and Commerce is
at the disposal of private corporations to study: (1) the market
conditions for new products, and (2) the technical possibilities
of producing these commodities. The Ministry is willing to

TABLE 42

INDUSTRIAL BREAKDOWN OF MANUFACTURING

Classification	Manufacturing Concerns
1) Primary Processing	a) Coffee Curing, b) Tobacco Processing, c) Sisal Processing, d) Tea Manufacture
2) Secondary Processing	a) Edible Oil Refining, b) Flour Milling, c) Food Canning, d) Sugar Manufacture, e) Tanneries
3) Goods Manufacture	a) Breweries, b) Goods Manufacture, c) Sugar Confectionary, d) Fruit Cordial Manufacture, e) Cotton Weaving, f) Pharmaceutical Manufacture, g) Rubber Processing, h) Soap Manufacture, i) Can Manufacture, j) Chemical Manufacture, k) Sheet Metal Works, l) Aluminum Manufacture
4) Building Materials Manufacture	a) Brick and Tile Manufacture, b) Nail Manufacture, c) Paint Manufacture, d) Cement Processing

TABLE 42--Continued

Classification	Manufacturing Concerns
5) Assembly	a) Air Conditioning, Refrigeration Equipment Assembly and Repair, b) Bicycle Assembly and Repair
6) Repair and Maintenance	a) Aircraft Maintenance, b) Electrical Repair, c) Locomotive and Rolling Stock Repairs, d) Tire Retreading
7) Service	a) Dry Cleaning, b) Laundering, c) Photographic Development, d) Servicing of Motor Vehicles
8) Basic Utilities	a) Electrical Power Generation, b) Ice Manufacture, c) Industrial Gas Manufacture, d) Water Supply
9) Other	a) Engineering--General and Marine, b) Scrap Metal Processing

Source: Arthur D. Little Report, pp. 19-21. See also Tanganyika, Statistical Abstract: 1962, Table L. 1, pp. 84-86; and IBRD, Table 75, pp. 476-77.

furnish to prospective investors such information as: (1) the availability of labor with appropriate skills, (2) the viability of the market, (3) the probability of granting rebates on import duties, and (4) the location and names of people in the country who will act as the suppliers of raw materials and the outlet for sales.

In most cases the initiative for obtaining this service rests upon the investor. The government did, however, initiate consultations with Iregal Textile Corporation of the United States with respect to establishing a plant in Tanganyika. In some cases the government invests funds in the undertaking. For example, it is a minority stockholder in a Portland cement factory at Wazo Hill near Dar Es Salaam. [48] In 1963, the government signed an agreement with the Italian State Oil Company. This firm agreed to build a ₺5 million oil refinery, and the government purchased one-half interest by granting the company exclusive refinery rights and providing ₺1.5 million in share capital. [49] The government also obtained 51 per cent of the firm Van Eeghen and Machine Ltd., and set up the International Trading and Credit Company of Tanganyika Ltd. (INTRATA) to advance the import and export wholesale business in conjunction with Cosata. [50] In 1966, the government announced that its share of INTRATA was about 90 per cent. [51]

✕What domestic private investment there is, is almost exclusively in the hands of the Asians. In many cases they have gone abroad at their own expense and initiative to form partnerships with foreign companies. For example, the Tanganyika Dye and Weaving Company is owned by Japanese and Asian interests, and the Tanganyika Enamel Houseware Company, which produces dishes and pottery, is jointly owned by Hong Kong and Asian investors. As yet, the Africans have not entered into this type of activity in any significant numbers. In order to induce the Africans to establish businesses, the government has established a fund whereby they can borrow small amounts at below market rates for capital purchases. The rate of interest charged is 5 per cent, while the market rate is about 10 to 15 per cent. The money, however, can only be used for the purchase of capital equipment; stocks for trade are excluded. To receive such a loan an African must invest an amount equal to one quarter of the total value of the enterprise in order to insure his

interest in the success of the venture. The type of enterprises
favored with these loans is small-scale operations such as
carpentry, the manufacture of household utensils, etc. After
four or five years in operation, the fund has only written off
the books as being lost about 3 per cent of the total amount
lent. [52]

The political leaders do not intend to rely solely upon
private initiative in order to establish a large manufacturing
sector. Two development corporations have been established
in order to promote and encourage large-scale manufacturing
activity. The purpose of these institutions is to attract foreign
funds as well as to create and operate governmentally-owned
enterprises, although no list of specific endeavors which they
plan to push has been published. The general areas of manufacturing carrying high priority status are, as stated, primary
processing and import-competing industries. Particular activities, however, are to be sponsored solely on an ad hoc basis.

One of the two development corporations--The National
Development Corporation (NDC)--is financed and controlled
solely by the government. The other--the Tanganyika Development Finance Corporation Limited (TDFL)--is semifree from
direct control of Tanganyika's government since it has been
financed by the governments of three nations. The NDC is a
statutory body which is scheduled to become a self-supporting,
semiautonomous institution in the forseeable future. In
order to establish its financial independence, the NDC is
interested in earning a profit on its investments, while at the
same time financing only those ventures which can be justified on grounds of promoting economic development.

The task which confronts the people of the NDC is immense. From 1962-70, it is estimated that the contribution
of the manufacturing sector to the gross domestic product
will increase by over 230 per cent. Total investment in manufacturing from 1964-69 is put at about Ł 60 million, of which
the government plans to spend about one-quarter. This projec-
tion of government investment plans amounts to a fifteen fold
increase from 1961-64 to 1964-69, while the NDC expects its
expenditures to increase by about thirty times during these
same two time periods. In 1964-65 alone, the NDC allocated
more funds to investment ventures than it planned during the
period covered by the Three-Year Plan. As for the other

three-quarters of the investment in manufacturing, this
corporation has been assigned a primary role in inducing
and assisting foreign private interests to invest in Tanganyika.

The major problems faced by the NDC officials are the
lack of profitable opportunities, a shortage of decision-making
talent, and the influence of political nationalism. These
problems will become evident by examining the NDC's operations. All applicants must initiate action by filling out an
application. The NDC then investigates the profitability of
the venture, judging this according to: (1) technical conditions of production, e.g., the availability of materials,
level of skill of management, etc.; and (2) the market demand. The following case study is an example of the procedures used. Mr. X is an Asian who requested a loan to
expand his tile and brick plant. The request was refused,
because: (1) Mr. X lacked experience in the manufacture of
tiles, and (2) the market demand was considered too small.

The primary reason for refusing the request of Mr. X
was the lack of sufficient demand. One government official
noted that this was the primary reason why four out of every
five requests are turned down. The market conditions for
Mangalore Tiles was such that one investigator estimated
that Mr. X could not operate his firm at over 30 per cent of
capacity. The type of investigation conducted is indicated in
the following statement by an official of NDC:

> There is currently no construction of the type house
> for which Mangalore tile is suitable. Mangalore tile
> roofs cost more than other types. This is particularly
> due to the high cost of substantial timbering necessary
> to support such roofs.

> The demand for Mangalore tile is particularly
> dependent upon the level of new building going on. But
> there are so many less expensive, highly satisfactory
> substitutes now. The development and availability of
> insulating materials has made flat slab roofs much
> more practical. However, there is a great demand
> for other clay products. [53]

According to the policy of the NDC, however, this investigator cannot suggest to the applicant that he produce other clay products for which there is a demand. The corporation fears that if the applicant accepts the recommendation, and then fails, he will blame them.

The investigator noted, in addition, that Mr. X lacked experience in the manufacture of Mangalore Tiles. He had no experience in operating a brick and tile plant, other than a very brief visit to one in India. He stated, further, that Mr. X had not demonstrated an ability to develop his present plant according to least cost principles.

The procedures for obtaining a loan not only involve a high degree of skill among the investigators, but among the applicants as well. If the borrower is able to provide security, he should fill out an application including: (1) a detached description of the manner in which he plans to utilize the funds, (2) an audited balance sheet for the current and prior years, and (3) an estimation of the operating costs with cash flow forecasts for the next three years.

A major problem confronting this corporation is how to deal with the increased political pressure being exerted in deciding which projects to finance. Political considerations are normally hidden under the general justification that indirect benefits are yielded to the economy through such investments. A major part of the problem is that the meaning of indirect benefits has not been precisely defined nor have procedures been outlined by which it can be measured. In many cases, the benefit that is to be received is not economic gain, but prestige for the nation. In other cases, indirect benefits are considered from the standpoint of only one segment of the population--the native Africans, i.e., some render indirect economic social benefits to the Africans at the expense of another race.

A major project which is being undertaken for prestige reasons is the construction of a cement plant near Dar Es Salaam. This plant will have a capacity of 130,000 tons per year. There are presently, however, three cement factories in East Africa, and all are operating at less than full capacity. The problem is that these three plants are located in Kenya and Uganda, and it is one of the few basic industries which can be profitably operated in Tanganyika.

Another of these projects is the development of game
reserves, whereby safaris can be operated at a relatively
low cost. At present, a private safari costs the hunter
approximately Ł1,000 to Ł1,500, while under the government's program this cost can be reduced to about Ł400.
The company is to be a joint venture, with the government
being the major shareholder and all rights for furnishing
transportation and hotel accommodations being leased to
private individuals. The profit, which will be derived from
the development of the land, however, is to accrue solely to
the landowner, which is the government.

The attitude of the political leaders toward private
enterprise emerged during the considerations of this project.
While one government official argued that private interests
should be included, because they would bring into the scheme
necessary managerial skills and capital, another opposed
this suggestion on grounds that complete governmental control
was the only way to prevent "economic exploitation." In the
final analysis, a compromise settlement was reached whereby
interests would be allowed to participate to the extent of
investing their capital. The total initial capital needed is
estimated at Ł140,000.

The problem with developing such a scheme is that
Uganda has already established one, and it appears highly
doubtful if East Africa can profitably support two of them.
One government official implied that the primary reason for
investing in this project was prestige and that certain political
leaders had exerted heavy pressure on the NDC to undertake
it. Arthur Sulzberger of the New York Times summarized the
attitude of the government in the following way: "It may take
two or three generations to haul the area out of its dreamy
past. Cities, airlines, and well-run game parks present a
twentieth-century facade that misrepresents reality."[54]

An example of a project which benefits the Africans at
the expense of another race is the establishment of a cooperative dairy in order to: (1) improve health, and (2) induce the
Africans to produce more milk. This scheme amounts to the
operation of a dairy processing plant. The firm will be
operated by private interests, although the NDC will be the
major stockholder. Eventually the NDC intends to sell its

holdings to the minority stockholder--The Tanganyika
Farmers' Cooperative Association (TFCA). UNICEF has
lent about Ł40,000 and an expert to install the equipment.
This loan is to be repaid over a ten-year period in the form
of free milk to children in hospitals and schools. The NDC
put up about Ł20,000 to be repaid at a rate of 7.5 per cent
over a ten year period with a five year moratorium, while
the TFCA bought Ł5,500 of equity in the venture. This firm
has been granted the exclusive right to process milk in its
area, which amounts to the elimination of the existing private Asian firms.

The repayment of the loan to UNICEF will be relatively
inexpensive because UNICEF has not specified the amount of
milk which must be delivered each month, only that it must
give Ł62,000 of free milk in a ten-year period, and the dairy
industry is faced with excess supplies during the year. This
annual excess is normally thrown away; thus the cost to the
firm could approach zero if the amount thrown away yearly
equalled Ł62,000 in a ten-year period.

Many people who apply for assistance are refused because their ventures are profitable enough to attract private
capital. The NDC is legally required to act as a lender of
last resort, i.e., to finance only those enterprises which
are too risky to be financed by private sources at a relatively
low rate of interest (5 per cent). For example, they considered a tea scheme which would involve a 12 to 15 per cent
rate to attract private funds. The reason that people with
profitable investment opportunities approach the NDC first,
especially if the investor is an Asian, is the desire to have
the government as a partner. The rationale is that this pro-
tects the investor from arbitrary decisions of government
officials, e.g., nationalization, as well as increases the
chances that the government will grant concessions, e.g.,
set lower prices on domestically produced agricultural products, grant exclusive privileges in the sale of goods through
licensing, etc.

Political leaders have been guilty of arbitrarily closing
certain businesses on personal grounds--especially hotels.
In 1962, Felix Anderson was given seven days to leave the
country for racially discriminating against Africans. [55] In
1963, the Safari Hotel in Arusha was ordered closed on

grounds that the proprietor had been discourteous to the
President of Guinea, Sekou Toure. The specific charges
were: (1) the manager did not greet his guest as he entered
the hotel, and (2) other guests (Europeans) did not rise when
the President entered. [56]

As to the creation of monopolies through industrial
licensing, the government has made this a policy. The
reason is not clear. The Ministry of Industry and Commerce
stated its policy in this manner: "While the legislation is
not designed to create monopolies, its object is to prevent
manufacturers of scheduled products from being subjected to
uneconomic competition within East Africa. "[57] The meaning
of the phrase uneconomic competition is not defined in this
report. B. M. Niculescu did, however, shed some light on
what the leaders mean:

> They (the governments of the nations in East and West
> Africa) have tended to consider the markets as an im-
> mutably fixed total, so that a larger share for one
> participant necessarily means a smaller share for
> some other participant. This static view, helped in
> individual cases by certain other fallacious "economic"
> theories and "facts" as well as by administrative con-
> venience, has rapidly led to a situation in which to
> "control, " that is ultimately and in practice to hamper
> trade, seems to have become the prime reason for all
> official measures in that context. [58]

The other corporation--the TDFL--was founded by three
governments in December, 1962: Tanganyika, Britain, and
West Germany. Each of these nations pledged Ł500,000 as
its initial capital. The aim is to create an international
development organization which would supplement the government's efforts in encouraging investment in Tanganyika:

> The sponsors believe that the role of private enterprise
> in the growth of the economy can be greatly expanded in
> a manner beneficial to the country if both local finance
> and local knowledge of business conditions can be made
> available to potential investors and industrialists. An
> organization (TDFL) has been formed which is capable
> of uniting experienced management and both local and
> overseas capital in worthwhile development projects. [59]

Their presumption is that the major obstacles to the
flow of foreign capital into Tanganyika is the lack of knowledge
of business conditions. Two more important limitations are:
(1) little confidence in the government, and (2) shortage of
profitable investment opportunities and complementary factors. The government has recognized the influence of (1),
and has made statutory guarantees against uncompensated
nationalization of private property. Foreign investors are
now issued certificates which allow them to transfer their
holdings out of Tanganyika, [60] if their firms are nationalized
as some were in February, 1967.

The government, as well as the TDFL, also speaks as
if the demand for capital is infinitely elastic, and that the
sole problem is one of supply. In this case, demand and
need are treated as being synonymous. The assertion does
not appear to be true, at least in the short run. Besides a
lack of aggregate demand, the absorption rate of the economy
is low, i.e., there is a lack of complementary factors and a
low level of technology. The Arthur D. Little Report noted
that Africa needs more technical aid than financial. [61] In
addition, there is a lack of trained labor.

The TDFL is not interested in mobilizing funds for
investment in social overhead capital or providing peasants
with short-term loans for the marketing of their crops. It is
solely interested in those forms of investments which yield a
profit. This corporation will provide financial assistance in
the form of medium or long-term loans, shareholdings or
debentures, as long as the profitability of the venture can be
shown. [62]

The criteria by which the TDFL decides the profitability
of a proposed investment is similar to that used, in principal,
by the NDC. They state: "Three principal matters must be
covered in the application: the credit standing and past
experience of sponsors, the long-range market for the product
and probable competition for that market, and the financial
details, including a forecast of capital and operating costs. "[63]
In other words, both the NDC and the TDFL emphasize: (1)
market demand, (2) experience of managers, and (3) financial
details of expenditure of loans. Unlike the NDC, however, the
TDFL does not offer government protection nor can direct
political pressure be exerted in influencing its decisions. In
its first three years, the company has lent about Ł1.4 million;

if the amount invested by its partners is included, the total amount invested is then about Ł 6 million.

In summary, a rapid rate of industrialization appears unlikely in the immediate future. The major form of manufacturing will remain processing for quite a time. Since this activity is dependent upon agriculture for its supply, the major obstacle is low agricultural productivity. As for the production of import-competing goods, Tanganyika's efforts are stymied by a small market (which again is directly related to an increase in agriculture) and poor technical conditions. In addition, the government's program is not as effective as it could be because of the emphasis on prestige projects. In conclusion, the industrialization of Tanganyika is going to be a fairly slow process.

CHAPTER **7** THE AVAILABILITY OF
CAPITAL FUNDS

The purpose of this chapter is to examine the sources
of capital funds which the planners intend to tap in financing
their development schemes. In so doing, we shall point out
that there is a small supply of domestic funds relative to
Tanganyika's projected development needs so that they are
relying mainly on foreign sources. This chapter is divided
into two parts: (1) domestic sources, and (2) foreign sources.

DOMESTIC SOURCES OF CAPITAL

The government's two means of mobilizing domestic
savings are: (1) taxing the incomes of individuals and businesses, and (2) borrowing from (a) East Africa's commercial
banks, (b) nonbanking financial intermediaries, and (c) the
cooperative movement.

Taxation

The major part of the government's revenue is collected
by taxation, and its relative importance has remained fairly
constant over the last ten years. For example, in 1954-55,
funds collected through taxation amounted to over 64 per cent
of the government's total revenue (recurrent and development
revenues), while in 1963-64, it accounted for less than 68 per
cent. The composition of tax revenues, on the other hand,
has changed. Indirect means of taxation, e. g., excise and
import, have increased in importance relative to direct, e. g.,
income taxation, during this same time period (Table 43).
The major reasons are the difficulties involved in levying
direct taxes on peasants' incomes: (1) a major part of their
total income is in the form of subsistence output, and it is
thus impossible to record; (2) there is a lack of such demographic information as births, deaths, occupation, place of
residence, etc.; and (3) the costs are high in physically collecting the revenue because of the scattered nature of African

145

TABLE 43

FUNDS COLLECTED BY TAXATION,
1954/55-1963/64

Year	Direct Taxation Ł thousands	Indirect Taxation Ł thousands	Indirect as a Per Cent of Total
1954/55	6,805	7,615	52.8
1955/56	6,315	8,136	56.3
1956/57	5,603	7,925	58.6
1957/58	6,061	8,603	58.7
1958/59	5,394	9,859	64.6
1959/60	5,561	11,470	67.4
1960/61	6,135	11,334	64.9
1961/62	6,073	11,712	65.9
1962/63	6,184	14,543	71.2
1963/64	7,080	16,617	70.1

Source: Tanganyika, Statistical Abstract: 1963, and Budget Survey 1965-66.

settlement. While such direct taxes as house or head yield
a relatively small part of the total tax revenues (in 1961/62
this category amounted only to 7 per cent), the indirect
effects are significant. These types of taxes force the African to seek monetary forms of employment since all tax payments in Tanganyika must be made in cash. In addition,
they do not affect marginal effort, and may even increase
total monetary activity if the African has an inelastic demand
for money.

The government faces a dilemma in raising funds
through taxation. While it needs investment funds, it desires,
at the same time, to avoid discouraging either the incentive
of private entrepreneurs to invest or the desire of the Africans
to work. This problem is summarized by the East Africa
Royal Commission:

> It is an essential theme of our Report that economic
> development in East Africa depends mainly on the
> enlargement of the market by the expansion of exports
> and local production and that public policy should be
> focused on the fulfillment of that end. This carries
> with it certain implications. New taxation which is
> added to an already heavy burden in order to provide
> revenue for otherwise desirable objects to social
> policy will, if it has the effect of checking the expan-
> sion of the economy, nullify its own purpose. On the
> other hand, an enlargement of the market will of itself
> tend to yield new revenue which in turn will provide
> the resources which governments require in order to
> develop their social policy. The weight of the argument
> thus lies on the side of lower rather than higher taxa-
> tion. Indeed, a general reduction in tax burdens, if
> they could be achieved, would contribute more to the
> economic development of the territories than any con-
> cessions which could be granted to privileged groups
> by means of tax rebates or subsidies. [1]

In line with this view, the policy has been to set export
taxes as low as possible in order to avoid discouraging this
type of activity. This excludes unavailable estimates of the
money withheld by cooperatives. As noted in Chapter 5, the
burden of these taxes falls completely on the peasant producer
who may well be on the margin of production. [2]

The forms of indirect taxation which raise the largest
amount of revenue are import duties and excise taxes; in
1961/62, they accounted for nearly 60 per cent of the total
tax revenue collected. [3] These duties are levied mainly on
such luxury items as beer, cigarettes, etc. in order to: (1)
protect competing goods produced within East Africa, and
(2) discourage the consumption of luxury goods and encourage
capital imports. Taxes collected on capital imports are
normally refunded upon request.

Because of the nature of Tanganyika's banking system,
the size of domestic borrowings is limited to the savings held
by the commercial banks and the non-banking financial intermediaries. Tanganyika's central bank amounts to a deposi-
tory of foreign exchange. It is unable to float bond issues
because of the lack of a capital market, or to borrow via
credit creation because the national currency is backed by
an equivalent amount of money held in pounds sterling. In
fact, because of this financial arrangement, Tanganyika is a
creditor nation, i.e., Tanganyika is actually lending funds to
foreign nations. This is caused by the necessity of maintaining a reserve of foreign securities, which can only be accumulated by maintaining an export surplus (see Table 44). It is
possible for Tanganyika to maintain this reserve in the short
run by borrowing from other nations. In the long run, however, this would make their money supply a function of other
governments' willingness to lend, and such a political dependence is clearly undesirable to the political leaders of
Tanganyika because of their fear of foreign domination.

The bank is then limited to lending only excess reserve
funds. There are at least two disadvantages to such a system:
(1) Tanganyika cannot realize its capital inflow potential, i.e.,
the nation must forego the opportunity to import necessary
capital equipment, and (2) there is the possibility that the
United Kingdom may devalue its currency, either by a deliberate
act of Parliament or by pursuing an inflationary monetary policy.
There are, on the other hand, several advantages, which make
it desirable over-all: (1) it acts as a restraint against the
temptation of introducing inflationary monetary policies and (2)
this arrangement puts Tanganyika on a hard currency system.
Both of these advantages facilitate its use of the international
market in promoting economic development.

TABLE 44

BALANCE OF TRADE, 1952-62
(£ thousands)

Year	Imports	Exports	Visible Balance of Trade
1952	37,495	47,413	+ 9,918
1953	28,427	35,610	+ 7,183
1954	31,962	37,774	+ 5,813
1955	43,531	37,413	- 6,618
1956	35,885	46,307	+10,422
1957	39,275	41,045	+ 1,771
1958	33,568	43,828	+10,260
1959	34,456	47,217	+12,762
1960	37,817	56,601	+18,784
1961	39,686	50,600	+10,914
1962	39,817	51,241	+11,424
		Net Reserves	+93,133

Source: Tanganyika, Statistical Abstract: 1963, Table E.1,
        p. 33.

Prior to Tanganyika's nationalization of its commercial banks, all of the commercial banks of East Africa operated as an integrated unit with Nairobi as the financial center (see Table 45). This complex was largely independent of direct governmental control in formulating investment and loan policies. These banks were in actuality foreign or expatriate banks, where a large percentage of their assets were held in the form of balances due from foreign banks. Most of their loans were for relatively short time periods, usually from 60-90 days. A large part of the reason was that the interest rate had been pegged through the initiative of the private bankers at a lower than market level in order to placate the East African governments. The interest rate charged was 7-8 per cent instead of a required 11-15 per cent to make long-term loans profitable. The bankers felt that if the market rates were used, then they would be subject to government intervention because the politicians would believe that the bankers were making exceptionally high profits by exploiting the poor African peasants. One banker noted that it was practically impossible to make long-term loans at interest rates of 7-8 per cent, unless the government secured the loan because of the risks involved. He stated, in fact, that he had never made, nor had he ever heard of, a mortgage loan being given. One important factor, then, leading to the recent nationalization of these banks, is probably the government's desire to gain control over the banks' investment decisions. For example, in 1962, only ₤700,000 were invested by all the banks of East Africa in this whole area; this amounts to 2 per cent of the total assets of all of these banks.[4]

Besides the pegging of the interest rate, an increase in long-term loans is hindered by a lack of available loanable funds which are short, partly because of: (1) political instability, and (2) a small supply of domestic savings. The political troubles in the Congo as well as the instability of the Asian population's position has led: (1) to capital flight, and (2) to a reduction in the inflow of foreign capital. At one point after independence, the price of brewery shares fell to the point where yields rose to over 20 per cent. Further, in order to meet the demand for agricultural marketing funds, one banker noted that he had to operate at times on as little as a 10 per cent reserve. From 1956 to 1961, withdrawals of Savings Banks exceeded deposits each year; in 1962 however, they were approximately equal, which is an indication that

TABLE 45

THE FLOW OF FUNDS
(£ thousands)

To/From	Nairobi	Dar Es Salaam	Kampala	London
Nairobi	--	4,705	7,525	3,075
Dar Es Salaam	5,639	--	825	681
Kampala	5,460	1,705	--	2,375
London	5,623	700	1,100	--

Source: Tanganyika, Statistical Abstract: 1962, Table 0.4,
         p. 103.

confidence was being restored by the new government. The
mutiny of 1963, however, destroyed this confidence quite a
bit, and serves to point out dramatically the precarious
position in which emerging nations find themselves with respect to maintaining attractive political conditions for private
investment. The effect of the nationalization of private enterprises in February, 1967, can only be harmful in this respect.

The small supply of domestic investment funds is in
large part explained by the reluctance of the native Africans
to hold their savings in commercial banks, because: (1) they
do not trust institutions which they do not understand, and
(2) they are myopic with respect to saving money for the
future. One banker stated, "The art of saving, as well as
the meaning of savings (money), is still new to the Africans."
In 1962, the total amount held in time and saving deposits in
all East African banks was only $7,846,000.[5] The govern-
ment has been attempting through exhortation to increase the
amount of money the Africans save. An official of the
government stated that if each worker saved twenty shillings
per month in the post office, the government would have
$385,000 per month more for development.[6] The results have
not, as yet, been promising.

The Asians have been hardest hit by the unstable political
situation in Tanganyika. Mr. P. Bomani, Minister for Finance,
noted that the decline in investment was in large part due to the
Asian's feeling of uncertainty as to what the future holds for
him.[7] The Asians have been sending their money to their
countries of origin for safekeeping since independence. In
1963 Erwin Blumenthal reported that capital flight was still
occurring;[8] and in 1966, Mr. Jamal, the new Minister for
Finance, announced that more restrictive measures on capital
outflow had been introduced.[9]

The government is also relying heavily on the use of
cooperative thrift societies as a means of mobilizing the
peasant Africans' savings. In 1960 there were no African
credit societies; by 1962, six had been established with a
total membership of eighty-one.[10] The slow growth was
remarked upon by one government official who said that the
Africans displayed no more trust in these governmentally
controlled institutions than in the commercial banks. As to
wage employees, the government has achieved greater success

in inducing savings. The national Provident Fund announced
that paid employees had saved close to Ł3 million with the
fund in 1965. [11]

FOREIGN SOURCES OF CAPITAL

Because of the limited tax base and the small supply of
domestic savings, the government has been forced to rely
rather heavily on foreign assistance in order to finance its
development program. In the Three-Year Plan, approximately
Ł19 million of the estimated development expenditure of Ł24
million, or over 80 per cent, was expected to be supplied from
foreign sources, [12] while about Ł117 million of the Five-Year
Plan's estimated expenditure of Ł246 million, or, over 50 per
cent, is expected to come from foreign sources. [13]

The two major sources of foreign funds are the United
Kingdom and the United States. From 1961-66, the governments of these two nations have furnished, or have pledged,
over Ł30 million; this amounts to over 80 per cent of the
funds from foreign sources that Tanganyika has received, or
expects to receive, during this period. While some of these
funds are grants (from 1961-69 Tanganyika expects about
Ł19 million in grants), [14] the major proportion is in the form
of low cost loans. United States funds are lent on a project
basis at a rate of 5 per cent, with a forty-year payoff period
and a ten-year moratorium, while West German funds are
lent at a rate of 5 per cent, with a twenty-year payoff period
and a five-year moratorium.

Two factors have provided major financial problems to
the planners: (1) funds pledged are not always forthcoming,
and (2) recurrent expenditures rise directly with capital
formation. While Ł19 million was pledged by foreign sources,
only about Ł11 million was received from 1961-64; this still
amounted to a little over 50 per cent of the total development
expenditure during this period. [15] The rise in recurrent
expenditure, as capital is created, is due to depreciation
charges and operating expenses. In the Three-Year Plan,
the capital to recurrent expenditure ratio was estimated at
0.38 per cent;[16] and from 1959-60 and 1965-66, recurrent
expenditure rose from Ł21,148,000 to Ł36,427,000, or by
about 70 per cent. [17]

Tanganyika's political leaders fear that this strong financial dependence could lead to a new form of political domination. In defense, they have adopted the rationale that Western nations owe economic aid to them as a payment for the years of economic exploitation which they experienced while under British domination. Julius Nyerere, in commenting on Tanganyika's slow rate of economic growth, stated that the present low rate was due to the Colonial powers having left their country "poor and with only land."[18] Mr. Karume, the First Vice-President, stated that the Western nations ought to lend to the underdeveloped countries funds, free of interest charges, as Red China was doing.[19]

In conclusion, Tanganyika is too financially poor to implement their development plan without large-scale foreign assistance. Their strong dependence on Western aid, however, has led the political leaders to react defensively toward their benefactors because of their fear of foreign domination.

CHAPTER **8** CONCLUSION

The purpose of this study was to examine the government's role in stimulating and promoting the process of economic development as well as speeding up the Africanization process. From the evidence, it appears that the political leaders have little faith in the ability of private entrepreneurs and a free market to achieve a high rate of economic growth, and they have turned to governmental leadership and economic planning. Tanganyika's form of planning does not involve complete governmental direction of investment and consumption expenditures, but is basically a method of setting guidelines and mobilizing resources to achieve certain economic goals. Tanganyika's political leaders have implemented their schemes on an ad hoc piecemeal basis; that is, no attempt has been made to eliminate all vestiges of private enterprise in one jump. However, African socialism, the accepted ideology, calls for the eventual complete substitution of government initiative for that of private enterprise and the consequent elimination of all sources of non-African economic power. The promotion of African nationalism, or the Africanization of Tanganyika's economic and political system, is as important a national aim as economic development; for the political leaders view the ownership of means of production by foreign nationals as a form of imperialism or as an extension of colonialism, i.e., the elite fears that foreign nationals will retain their political power through the ownership of the means of production. The leaders' aim is to restrict the use of this power by government regulation and statutory monopolies.

The speed with which the government is moving to eliminate the non-African's power is limited by the nature of the economic system and the need of outside assistance in order to increase the rate of economic growth. As indicated in this study, Tanganyika is poor with respect to its natural resource and population base. A small percentage of its land area is used in agricultural production, and the major part of this is

155

used in low-productivity peasant farming. There are presently
no economically accessible basic minerals that can attract private investment funds and provide the foundation for large-
scale industrial growth. The small size of the market, the
general shortage of necessary social overhead capital, and the
lack of an adequately trained labor supply make all forms of
large-scale manufacturing activity unattractive. The structure
of the economy makes nonsensical any notion that Tanganyika
can become fairly economically independent in the near future.
Tanganyika is dependent upon foreign trade for earning money
income and importing capital equipment. In addition, the
shortage of domestic investment funds, relative to its planned
development expenditure, results in a strong dependence on
foreign sources of capital.

Europeans who reside in Tanganyika have also provided
the government with valuable assistance: directly, by aiding
in the commercialization of African agriculture, and, indirectly, by creating nonagricultural forms of employment in Tanganyika's major manufacturing industry, sisal. For this
reason, a sort of truce between the Europeans and the government has been established. The immediate future of the Asians
looks less hopeful than that of the Europeans. The political
elite view the Asian traders as an impediment to the increase
in the African's participation in commercial activities, rather
than as an aid. They claim that the Asians have formed a
"closed shop" in commercial activities in order to exclude the
African, as well as to exploit him.

The method of eliminating the Asian dominance is in
keeping with the political leaders' accepted ideology. There
has been no attempt to create an African business class which
would have the responsibility for organizing economic activity
in a free market. Emphasis has been placed instead on establishing a governmentally dominated cooperative movement,
which amounts to a system of state-regulated trade. The
reason is that the leaders do not believe that trade leads to an
extension of the market, i.e., that trade acts as a catalyst in
the growth process. They believe instead that it is simply an
appendage to the production process, and thus that private
trade can be eliminated without any harmful effects on the
rate of economic growth.

The cooperative form of organization is the sole means now used to carry on agricultural trading activities. At the present time, cooperatives are used primarily to market the crops produced by native Africans; in the future, however, this form of organization will replace the Asians in wholesale and retail trade. The reasons that the political leaders chose cooperatives are threefold: (1) there is no existing African private entrepreneurial class; (2) tribal society is collective in nature, and it is hoped that cooperatives, which are based on collective principles and have been formed along tribal lines, will be readily accepted by the native Africans and easily adaptable to the existing tribal system; and (3) cooperatives are an organization in which all Africans can derive feelings of participation, but which the government can easily control through a pyramidal organizational structure.

The effect of governmental action on the rate of economic growth is difficult to assess accurately. The leaders desire to double the 1954-62 rate of economic growth in the period 1964-69. The major obstacle lies in the agricultural sector. This sector's output constitutes about 60 per cent of Tanganyika's gross domestic product and accounts for about 90 per cent of the working population. The main problem in increasing agricultural output is the large proportion of economic activity which goes into subsistence production. This type of activity accounts for approximately 50 per cent of agricultural output and two-thirds to three-fourths of the agricultural land. Subsistence production is normally performed in a tribal setting under native laws and customs.

Tribal laws and customs are major obstacles to economic progress. They emphasize the maximization of the common good through the use of egalitarian principles in the division of tribal means of production. One form of this is the land tenure laws, which lead in most cases to a divergence in the use of tribal resources between social and private costs. For example, the range land of many tribes is communally owned, and there is no cost to the individual members of the tribe for the use of this land. There is then an incentive for each individual to graze as many cows as possible on this land, because the livestock herds are individually owned. The results are an overstocking of the range, i.e., too high a ratio of livestock to land, leading to a deterioration of the soil's fertility.

Still another example is the system of cultivatable land distribution practiced by many native authorities. The land is divided equally among the tribal members in line with the custom of giving each member an equal share of the group's wealth. An attempt is even made sometimes to grant to each member an equal amount of each grade of land which the tribe possesses. The result is that people hold their land in strips, making inefficient the use of more advanced types of capital, e.g., tractors. In addition, since ownership does not reside with the individual, there is no incentive to protect the land from soil erosion, and a system of shifting cultivation is used. Shifting cultivation is an obstacle to the accumulation of fixed forms of capital since the African intends to abandon the land he is currently using. Even if tribal institutions were eliminated, the structure of agricultural activity would still provide obstacles to growth. There is presently a small supply of investment funds, a low level of technology, and a dearth of skills. The likelihood, however, that these impediments could be overcome, would be increased by the elimination of institutions which do not emphasize individual gain in material terms.

If manufacturing activity is to be increased at a rapid rate, major obstacles must be overcome: (1) the low level of per capita income which indicates the low level of aggregate demand; (2) a large export sector, which restricts the use of autarkic policies to protect the existing internal market for domestic producers; (3) the backwash effects that have occurred from Tanganyika's attempts to expand the size of its internal market through a common market arrangement with Kenya and Uganda; (4) a general shortage of social overhead capital; (5) a labor supply which is unskilled, undisciplined, and unstable; and (6) a shortage of managerial skills. At present, the structure of this sector is orientated toward processing, with sisal accounting for over 30 per cent of manufacturing's labor force. The government has been instrumental in the organization of two development corporations whose objective is to encourage the establishment of secondary industry. In addition, the use of industrial licensing has been used as a means of protecting the market for privileged producers. As of yet, the efforts of these corporations have not been noteworthy. The main stumbling blocks are the lack of profitable investment opportunities, the influence of political nationalism, and the inadequate supply of skilled managers.

In the final analysis, the problem is so immense that one cannot expect amazing results from the government's efforts. It appears highly doubtful that the technical conditions will permit a substantial increase in the rate of economic growth in the forseeable future. In addition, the approach of the government to Tanganyika's development problems is questionable. At a time when there is an acute shortage of decision-making talent, the leaders have sought to substitute a government machinery for a price mechanism to allocate resources, as well as to Africanize all key positions in the economy. As stated, the official view of a free market is that it is an appendage to the production process and that a price system is an unnecessary luxury. Such a view overlooks the great value that a price system can play in maximizing the use of decision-making talent and generating change.

NOTES

NOTES TO INTRODUCTION

1. *African Diary*, December 16-21, 1961, p. 295; and *Kessing's Contemporary Archives, Weekly Diary of World Events*, December 2-9, 1961, p. 18473.

2. United Nations, *Yearbook of the United Nations, 1961* (United Nations, Lake Success: Office of Public Information, 1961), p. 727.

3. Technically, TANU candidates were only elected to ten out of thirty available seats, because the election law required each person to vote for an African, a European, and an Asian candidate. The Europeans and Asians elected, however, were all TANU backed. *Kessing's*, March 28-April 4, 1959, p. 16723.

4. In the general election of 1960, TANU candidates captured seventy of the seventy-one available seats. The lone seat was won by H. E. Sarwatt, an independent and son of the chief of the largest tribe in the district--Iraqw. *Ibid.*, December 8-15, 1962, p. 19132.

5. He polled 97 per cent of the vote in the 1962 elections. *Ibid.*, September 5-12, 1962, p. 17666.

6. Julius K. Nyerere, *Democracy and the Party* (Dar Es Salaam: Tanganyika Standard, 1962); Julius K. Nyerere, "African Nationalism," *African Quarterly*, III (1963), pp. 115-21; and Julius K. Nyerere, "Will Democracy Work in Africa?" *Africa Special Report*, V (February, 1960), pp. 3-4. See also the United Republic of Tanzania, *Report of the Presidential Commission on the Establishment of a Democratic One Party State* (Dar Es Salaam: Government Printer, 1965).

7. Nyerere, *Democracy and the Party*; and Fred G. Burke, "Tanganyika: The Search for Ujama," *African Socialism*, ed. William H. Friedland and Carl G. Rosberg, Jr. (Stanford: Stanford University Press, 1964), p. 219.

8. Nyerere, Democracy and the Party, p. 15.

9. African Recorder, August 27-September 9, 1962, p. 268.

10. Ibid.

11. Ibid., January 29-February 11, 1963, p. 397.

12. Ibid. See also Presidential Commission Report.

13. Presidential Commission Report, pp. 15-16. See also Nyerere, Democracy and the Party.

14. African Diary, March 4-10, 1963, p. 1137.

15. African Recorder, February 26-March 10, 1964, p. 718.

16. Presidential Commission Report.

17. Tanganyika Standard, March 26, 1964, p. 5.

18. African Recorder, March 26-April 8, 1962, p. 133.

19. Ibid., August 17-September 9, 1962, p. 268.

20. Ibid., November 5-18, 1962, p. 326.

21. Presidential Commission Report, p. 26.

22. Arthur O. Sulzberger claims that Tanganyika is presently being ruled dictatorially by a political group of about 400 people. The New York Times, March 30, 1964, p. 28. For a discussion of the political structure of Tanganyika, see Margaret Bates, "Tanganyika," African One-Party States, ed. Gwendolen M. Carter (Ithaca, N.Y.: Cornell University Press, 1962), pp. 395-479.

23. See H. M. Smythe and M. M. Symthe, "The Nigerian Elite: Some Observations," Sociology and Social Research (September-October, 1959), pp. 42-45; J. E. Goldthorpe, "An African Elite," British Journal of Sociology, VI (March, 1955), pp. 31-47; Edward Shils, "Political Development in the New States," Comparative Studies in Society and History, IV (April, 1960), pp. 265-292; K. A. Busia,

"The Present Situation and Aspirations of Elites in The
Gold Coast, " International Social Science Bulletin, VIII
(1956), pp. 424-431; and P. Mercier, "Evolution of
Senegalese Elites, " International Social Science Bulletin,
VIII (1956), pp. 441-452.

24. Goldthorpe, "African Elite, " pp. 31-47.

25. Shils, "Political Development, " p. 272.

26. T. O. Beidelman describes the hostility involved in
    intertribal rivalry in East Central Tanganyika. T. O.
    Beidelman, "Intertribal Insult and Opprobrium in an
    East African Chiefdom, " Anthropological Quarterly,
    XXXVII (April, 1964), pp. 33-52.

27. See Nyerere, "African Nationalism, " pp. 115-121; and
    Nyerere, "Will Democracy Work in Africa?" pp. 3-4.

28. Burke, "Tanganyika, " p. 205.

29. It refers to the collective ownership of the means of
    production to insure a less unequal distribution of income.
    Joseph Schumpeter, Capitalism, Socialism, and Democ-
    racy (3rd ed.; New York: Harper and Brothers, 1950),
    p. 167; and Calvin B. Hoover, The Economy, Liberty
    and The State (New York: Doubleday and Company, 1961),
    pp. 11-27.

30. See Bethwell A. Ogot, "Deviation is Inherent, " East
    Africa Journal (April, 1964), pp. 2-6; John Kakonge,
    "Scientific Socialism in Africa, " East Africa Journal
    (April, 1964), pp. 6-9; and William H. Friedland and
    Carl G. Rosberg, Jr., "The Anatomy of African Social-
    ism, " African Socialism, pp. 1-11.

31. John B. George, "How Stable is Tanganyika?" Africa
    Report, VIII (March, 1963), p. 3.

32. Kakonge, "Scientific Socialism, " p. 8. For a similar
    explanation of why African trade unions do not affiliate
    with those of Eastern and Western countries, see K. S.
    Musisi, "The Role of African Governments: 'Supervision'
    or 'Control'?" Africa Report (June, 1965), p. 19.

33. Ogot, "Deviation, " p. 6.

34. Nyerere, "Will Democracy Work in Africa?" pp. 3-4.

35. For a similar view, see Friedland and Rosberg, "The Anatomy of African Socialism, " pp. 5-7; and Chandler Morse, "The Economics of African Socialism, " African Socialism, pp. 35-52.

36. The United Republic of Tanganyika and Zanzibar, Five-Year Plan for Economic and Social Development, 1st July, 1964-30th June, 1969, Vol. I (Dar Es Salaam: Government Printer, 1964), p. 79.

37. African Recorder, February 12-25, 1964, p. 702.

38. Ibid., September 10-23, 1963, p. 571.

39. See remarks by Paul Bomani, Minister for Finance, African Recorder, February 26-March 10, 1964, p. 718; and Michael Kamaliza, Minister for Labor, African Diary, October 19-25, 1963, p. 1403.

40. African Diary, October 19-25, 1963, p. 1403.

41. African Recorder, February 12-25, 1964, p. 411.

42. See P. T. Bauer and B. S. Yamey, The Economics of Under-Developed Countries (Cambridge: James Nisbet and Company, 1957), pp. 16-31; African Studies in Income and Wealth, ed. L. H. Samuels (Chicago: Quadrangle Books, 1963); and Mark Karp, The Economics of Trusteeship in Somalia (Toston: Boston University Press, 1960), pp. 19-37.

NOTES TO CHAPTER 1

1. Tanganyika, Statistical Abstract: 1963 (Dar Es Salaam:

Government Printer, 1963), p. 1; J. P. Moffett (ed.),
Handbook of Tanganyika (Dar Es Salaam: Government
Printer, 1958), p. 1; and J. F. R. Hill, Tanganyika, A
Review of Its Resources and Their Development, ed.
J. P. Moffett (Norwich, England: Jarrold and Sons,
1955), p. 15.

2. Moffett, Handbook, p. 5; and A. H. Saville, "African
   Agriculture in Tanganyika Territory," East African
   Agriculture, ed. J. K. Matheson and E. W. Bovill
   (London: Oxford University Press, 1950), p. 237.

3. International Bank for Reconstruction and Development,
   The Economic Development of Tanganyika (Baltimore:
   Johns Hopkins Press, 1961), p. 18.

4. IBRD, p. 17; and East Africa, Royal Commission, 1953-
   55 Report, CMD. 9475 (London: HMSO, 1955), p. 254.

5. "Topography," East African Agriculture, p. 4.

6. Moffett, Handbook, pp. 2-5.

7. See IBRD, p. 17; and EARC, 1953-55 Report, p. 254.

8. This area, however, is infested with the tsetse fly.

9. Tanganyika, Statistical Abstract: 1963, p. 3.

10. Moffett, Handbook, p. 155.

11. IBRD, p. 17.

12. Moffett, Handbook, p. 4.

13. See Hill, A Review, p. 245; and Great Britain, the
    Economist Intelligence Unit, The Economy of East
    Africa, 1955, p. 186.

14. The estimated cost is about $140 million. Aron Segal,
    "The Tanganyika-Zambia Railway Project," Africa
    Report, IX (November, 1964), pp. 9-10.

15. IBRD, pp. 12 and 50-52.

16. United Nations, Demographic Yearbook: 1962 (New York: United Nations, 1962), p. 26.

17. United Nations, Economic and Social Council, Economic Commission for Africa, Seminar on Population Problems in Africa, Population Distribution, Internal Migration and Urbanization in Africa (E/CN. 14/ASPP/L. 3-E/CN. 9/ CONF. 3/63)(Cairo: United Nations, 1962), p. 8.

18. Richard W. Stephens, Population Pressures in Africa South of the Sahara (Washington, D.C.: George Washington University, 1959), p. 12.

19. United States, Bureau of the Census, Statistical Abstract of the United States, 1964.

20. United Nations, Economic Commission for Africa, Economic Bulletin for Africa, II (June, 1962), p. 62.

21. See EARC, 1953-55 Report, pp. 201-203; Economic Bulletin for Africa, II (June, 1962), p. 63; Hugh H. Smith, "Urbanization in Nigeria," Anthropological Quarterly (July, 1960), pp. 143-148; and John Friedman, "Cities in Social Transformation," Comparative Studies in Society and History, IV (November, 1961), pp. 86-103.

22. This problem is aggravated by the ability of Africans to live off fellow tribal members after they have become unemployed and are not earning sufficient income to support themselves. See J.A.K. Leslie, A Survey of Dar Es Salaam (London: Oxford University Press, 1960), p. 10.

23. Tanganyika Standard, May 12, 1964, pp. 2-3.

24. Salaka Hussun and William Maulidi were sentenced to three months in prison for returning to Dar Es Salaam after they had been banned. Tanganyika Standard, September, 1963, p. 3.

25. Economic Bulletin for Africa, II (June, 1962), p. 64.

26. $\dfrac{\text{Number of people 0-15 and 65 and over}}{\text{Number of people 15-65}}$ = dependency ratio

27. For a discussion of this factor, see Gerald Meier and
    Robert Baldwin, Economic Development (New York:
    John Wiley and Sons, 1959), pp. 283-284; Stephen Enke,
    Economics for Development (New Jersey: Prentice Hall,
    1963), pp. 357-358; and John D. Durand, "Population
    Structure as a Factor in Manpower and Dependency
    Problems of Under-Developed Countries," Population
    Bulletin (New York: United Nations, October, 1953),
    pp. 1-16.

28. For a discussion of this aspect in a tribe in Southern
    Tanganyika, see Kumbert Lussy, "Some Aspects of Work
    and Recreation Among the Wakagoro of Southern Tangan-
    yika," Anthropological Quarterly (October, 1963), pp.
    109-128; in tropical Africa, see William Barber, The
    Economy of British Central Africa (Stanford: Stanford
    University Press, 1961), pp. 193-194; and D. Hobart
    Houghton, "Migrant Labour," Africa in Transition, ed.
    Prudence Smith (London: Max Reinhardt, 1958), p. 44;
    for a general discussion, see P. T. Bauer and B. S.
    Yamey, "Economic Progress and Occupational Distribu-
    tion," The Economic Journal, LXI (December, 1951), pp.
    741-755.

29. Tanganyika, Employment and Earnings in Tanganyika 1961
    (Dar Es Salaam: Government Printer, 1962); United
    Nations, Economic Survey of Africa Since 1950 (E/CN.
    14228) (New York: United Nations, 1959), p. 43; and
    M. J. B. Molohan, Detribilization (Dar Es Salaam: Govern-
    ment Printer, 1959), p. 13.

30. EARC, 1953-55 Report, pp. 153-156; J. E. Goldthorpe,
    Outlines of East African Society (Kampala, Uganda:
    Makerere College, 1959), pp. 146-161; and P. H. Gulliver,
    Labour Migration in a Rural Society (Kampala, Uganda:
    East African Institute of Social Research, 1955).

31. This amounts to 150,000 workers out of about 400,000 in
    Tanganyika. Gulliver, Labour Migration, p. ii. M.
    Yudelman estimates that between 45 and 50 per cent of
    Northern Rhodesia's labor force is composed of migratory
    people. Montague Yudelman, Africans on the Land
    (Cambridge: Harvard University Press, 1964), p. 1.

32. Goldthorpe referred to these workers as target-workers, while one Tanganyikan government official referred to this type of employment as target employment. Goldthorpe, Outlines of East African Society, p. 151.

33. EARC, 1953-55 Report, p. 201.

34. See Walter Elkan, "Some Social Policy Implications of Industrial Development in East Africa," International Social Science Journal, XVI (1964), pp. 390-400; and Walter Elkan, Migrants and Proletarians (London: Oxford University Press, 1960), p. 136.

35. EARC, 1953-55 Report, pp. 153-154; and Yudelman, Africans on the Land, p. 131.

36. For a discussion of the effects of education on economic growth, see Theodore W. Schultz, "Capital Formation by Education," Journal of Political Economy, LXVIII (January, 1960), pp. 571-583; and Andrew F. Frank, "Human Capital and Economic Growth," Economic Development and Cultural Change, VIII (January, 1960), pp. 170-173.

37. Economic Bulletin for Africa, II (June, 1962), p. 19.

38. Betty George, Education for Africans in Tanganyika (Washington, D.C.: United States Department of Health, Education and Welfare, 1960), p. 8.

39. Tanganyika, Statistical Abstract: 1963, pp. 166-167.

40. The United Republic of Tanganyika and Zanzibar, Tanganyika Five-Year Plan for Economic and Social Development, 1st July, 1964-30th June, 1969, Vol. I (Dar Es Salaam: Government Printer, 1964), pp. 13 and 82. See also, for a discussion of how these estimates were determined, George Tobias, High-Level Manpower Requirements and Resources in Tanganyika 1962-67 (Dar Es Salaam: Government Printer, 1963); and Robert L. Thomas, Survey of the High-Level Manpower Requirements and Resources for the Five-Year Plan 1964/65 to 1968/69 (Dar Es Salaam: Government Printer, 1965).

41. Guy Hunter, Education for a Developing Region (London: George Allen and Unwin, 1962), p. 59.

42. Tanganyika, Statistical Abstract: 1963, p. 168.

43. African Diary, January 25-31, 1964, pp. 1571-1572.

44. Tanganyika, Development Plan for Tanganyika 1961/62-1963/64 (Dar Es Salaam: Government Printer, 1962), p. 81.

45. Five-Year Plan 1964-69, Vol. I, p. 67.

46. African Diary, January 25-31, 1964, p. 1571.

47. The government intends to increase the number of students entering the University of East Africa by 200 per cent from 1964-69. Five-Year Plan 1964-69, Vol. I, p. 67.

48. P. Evans notes that this trend is not due to higher education being antirural in nature, i.e., farming being less prestigious than other occupations. Education, however, has led to a rise in the expectations of the Africans for higher levels of living, and such a goal could not presently be attained in farming or will be slow in coming through government efforts. P.C.C. Evans, "Western Education and Rural Productivity in Tropical Africa," Africa (October, 1962), pp. 313-323.

49. African Recorder, December 17-31, 1963, p. 658.

NOTES TO CHAPTER 2

1. A.Z.N. Swai, Minister for Economic Planning, "Approach to Economic Planning," The United Republic of Tanganyika and Zanzibar, Tanganyika Five-Year Plan for Economic and Social Development, 1st July, 1964-30th June, 1969, Vol. I (Dar Es Salaam: Government Printer, 1964), pp. 1-4.

2. See Ferdynand Zweig, The Planning of Free Societies (London: Secker and Warburg, 1942), pp. 11-17.

3. For a case study of planning in African countries, see Barbu Niculescu, Colonial Planning (London: George Allen and Unwin, 1958).

4. Tanganyika, Development Plan for Tanganyika 1961/62-1963/64 (Dar Es Salaam: Government Printer, 1962).

5. Ibid. , p. 1.

6. Ibid. , pp. 7-8.

7. Tanganyika, Budget Survey, 1964-65 (Dar Es Salaam: Government Printer, 1964), p. 17; and Tanganyika, Budget Survey, 1965-66, pp. 36-37.

8. Tanganyika Standard, May 13, 1964, p. 1.

9. Five-Year Plan 1964-69, Vol. I, p. viii.

10. Ibid. , pp. viii-ix.

11. In reality, the government intends to increase gradually the yearly expenditure on development during the period of this plan.

12. Five-Year Plan 1964-69, Vol. I, p. 1.

13. Tanganyika, Budget Survey, 1965-66, pp. 36-37.

14. Ibid. , pp. xv-xvi.

NOTES TO CHAPTER 3

1. Tanganyika, The Gross Domestic Product of Tanganyika 1954-57 (Dar Es Salaam: Government Printer, 1959), p. 2; and Alan T. Peacock and Douglas G. M. Dosser, The National Income of Tanganyika 1952-54 (Colonial Research Study, No. 26; London: HMSO, 1958), pp. 6-10. These were the first works on national accounts in Tanganyika. Also, see T. A. Kennedy, H. W. Ord, and David Walker, "On the Calculation and Interpretation of National Accounting in East Africa, " African Studies in

Income and Wealth, ed. L. H. Samuels (Chicago: Quadrangle Books, 1963), pp. 357-360.

2. Gross Domestic Product of Tanganyika 1954-57, p. 6.

3. Tanganyika, Budget Survey, 1964-65 (Dar Es Salaam:
   Government Printer, 1964), p. 3.

4. A. R. Prest and I. G. Stewart, The National Income of
   Nigeria 1950-52 (Colonial Research Studies No. 11;
   London: HMSO, 1953), p. 10.

5. Anthropologists do not agree on whether bride-price is
   an economic or social payment, or some combination of
   both. It is agreed, however, that a man must make such
   a payment in order to acquire these rights in a wife. See
   Robert F. Gray, "Sonjo Bride-Price and the Question of
   African 'Wife Purchase'," American Anthropologist, 62
   (February, 1960), pp. 34-57; and Phillip Gulliver,
   "Bride-Wealth: The Economic vs. The Noneconomic
   Interpretation," American Anthropologist, 63 (1961),
   pp. 1098-1100.

6. The National Income of Tanganyika 1952-54, p. 15.

7. The Gross Domestic Product of Tanganyika 1954-57.

8. The National Income of Tanganyika 1952-54, p. 22.

9. C. J. Martin, "The Development and Diversity of National
   Income Series in East Africa Since 1947," American
   Studies in Income and Wealth, p. 342.

10. See The National Income of Tanganyika 1952-54, pp. 22-35;
    and The Gross Domestic Product of Tanganyika 1954-57,
    pp. 9 and 35.

11. United Nations, Report by a Group of Experts, Report on
    International Definition and Measurement of Standards and
    Levels of Living (E/cn. 3/179E/cn. 299) (New York: United
    Nations, March, 1954), p. 2.

12. For a discussion of this point, see The National Income of
    Tanganyika 1952-54, pp. 48-49; The National Income of

Nigeria 1950-52, p. 81; S. Herbert Frankel, "Concepts of Income and Welfare--In Advanced and Developed Societies--With Special Reference to the Inter-Comparability of National Income Aggregates," Income and Wealth, Series III, ed. Milton Gilbert (Cambridge: Bowes and Bowes, 1953), pp. 156-168; and United Nations, Statistical Papers, Per Capita National Product of Fifty-five Countries: 1952-54 (Series E, No. 4; New York: United Nations, 1957), pp. 9-10.

13. Statistical Papers (Series E, No. 1), pp. 9-10; and Statistical Papers (Series E, No. 4, 1957), p. 4.

14. The National Income of Tanganyika 1952-54, p. 49.

15. Tanganyika, Statistical Abstract: 1962 (Dar Es Salaam: Government Printer, 1962), p. 16.

16. The Gross National Product of Tanganyika 1954-57, pp. 82-83.

17. Ibid., p. 15.

18. The National Income of Nigeria 1950-52, p. 2.

19. The National Income of Tanganyika 1952-54, p. 10.

20. The Gross Domestic Product of Tanganyika 1954-57, p. 15.

21. Simon Kuznets, "Quantitative Aspects of the Economic Growth of Nations: VI Long-term Trends in Capital Formation Proportions," Economic Development and Cultural Change, IX (July, 1961), p. 4.

22. There are strong grounds for accepting this observation, since historically it has been found that peasant agricultural communities have a fairly constant labor:capital ratio. See Colin Clark and Margaret Haswell, The Economics of Subsistence Agriculture (London: Macmillan and Company, 1964), pp. 69-94.

23. This coincides with the findings of Montague Yudelman. He notes that wage employment in Northern Rhodesia has

been increasing at a rate of 7 per cent per annum. Since
1956, however, the number of workers in wage employment has remained fairly constant. Montague Yudelman,
Africans on the Land (Cambridge: Harvard University
Press, 1964), p. 136.

24. Tanganyika, Annual Labor Report 1954 and 1958; Tangan-
    yika, Statistical Abstract: 1962, p. 145; and Tanganyika,
    Budget Survey 1965-66, p. 27.

25. Tanganyika Standard, June 15, 1966, p. 2.

26. Ibid., May 12, 1964, p. 3. See, for a general discussion,
    Walter Elkan, "Some Policy Implications of Industrial
    Development in East Africa, " International Social Science
    Journal, XVI (1964), p. 396.

27. United Nations, Economic Survey of Africa Since 1950
    (E/CN. 14228) (New York: United Nations, 1959), p. 99.

28. Ibid.

29. The work force, in peasant agriculture, is held to be a
    relatively constant percentage of the total population
    engaged in peasant farming.

NOTES TO CHAPTER 4

1. The group grown mainly for subsistence is the basic food
   crops; this includes: (1) rice, (2) maize, (3) millet, (4)
   sorghums, (5) beans and peas, and (6) cassava (root).

2. United Nations, Economic Survey of Africa Since 1950
   (E/CN. 14228) (New York: United Nations, 1959), p. 100;
   and Commodity Yearbook 1964 (New York: Commodity
   Research Bureau, 1964), p. 166.

3. See Sayre P. Schatz, "A Dual-Economy Model of an Under-
   developed Country, " Social Research, XXIII (Winter, 1956);
   and J. H. Boecke, Economics and Economic Policy of Dual
   Societies (New York: Institute of Pacific Relations, 1953).

4. Great Britain, Tanganyika Under United Kingdom Administration: 1960, Part 1 (London: HMSO, 1960), pp. 61-62.

5. Ibid.

6. Kathleen M. Stahl, Tanganyika, Sail in the Wilderness
   (Netherlands: Moulton and Company, 1961), pp. 46-47.

7. International Bank for Reconstruction and Development,
   The Economic Development of Tanganyika (Baltimore:
   Johns Hopkins Press, 1961), p. 201.

8. Ibid. For a discussion on the uncertainty of the effects of
   foreign enclaves on the agricultural practices of Africans,
   in Kenya, see Eric Clayton, "A Note on the Alien Enclave
   and Development;" and T. C. I. Ryan, "A Rejoinder to Dr.
   Clayton's Note on the Alien Enclave and Development, "
   East African Economics Review, X (June, 1963), pp. 35-46.

9. Tanganyika, Statistical Abstract: 1962 (Dar Es Salaam:
   Government Printer, 1962), pp. 85-86.

10. Tanganyika, Census of Large Scale Commercial Farming
    in Tanganyika 1960 (Kenya: East African Statistical
    Department, June, 1961), p. 12.

11. IBRD, p. 205.

12. Tanganyika Sisal Growers Association, Annual Report 1964-
    65 (Dar Es Salaam: Tanganyika Standard Ltd., 1965), p. 14.

13. See Tanganyika, Report of the Minimum Wages Board (Dar
    Es Salaam: Government Printer, 1962).

14. Trade Disputes (Arbitration and Settlement Ordinance,
    Cap. 296).

15. Tanganyika, Annual Labor Report 1961; and Tanganyika
    Standard, May 23, 1964, p. 2.

16. Tanganyika, Labor Report 1961; and Report on the State of
    Industrial Relations in the Sisal Industry (Dar Es Salaam:
    Government Printer, 1958), p. 2.

17. Then called the Tanganyika Federation of Unions.

18. African Diary, January 26-February 1, 1964, p. 976; and African Diary, March 30-April 5, 1963, p. 1081.

19. Tanganyika Sisal Growers Association, Annual Report 1964-65, pp. 14-15.

20. IBRD, pp. 205-206; and Stahl, Sail, p. 41.

21. Stahl, Sail, p. 44.

22. Tanganyika Under United Kingdom Administration: 1960, pp. 60-62.

23. Ibid., pp. 59-61.

24. See Hugh Foot, "Whites in Africa," Saturday Review (July 25, 1964), pp. 10-12; and Tanganyika Standard, June 15, 1966, pp. 3-4.

25. Tanganyika, Ministry for Commerce and Industry, Annual Report of the Commerce and Industry Division 1963 (Dar Es Salaam: Government Printer, 1964), p. 1.

26. Tanganyika Standard, May 13, 1964, p. 3.

27. African Diary, February 1-7, 1964, p. 1583.

28. African Recorder, February 15-25, 1962, p. 94.

29. Proposals of the Tanganyika Government for Land Tenure Reform (Government Paper No. 2; Dar Es Salaam: Government Printer, 1962), p. 1.

30. Ibid., p. 3.

31. IBRD, pp. 94-95.

32. The United Republic of Tanganyika and Zanzibar, Five-Year Plan for Economic and Social Development, 1st July, 1964-30th June, 1969, Vol. I (Dar Es Salaam: Government Printer, 1964), p. 23.

33. Tanganyika Standard, September 11, 1964, p. 1.

34. Tanganyika Standard, April 23, 1964, p. 5; and Tanganyika Sisal Growers Association, Annual Report 1964-65, p. 8.

35. Tanganyika, Development Plan for Tanganyika 1961/62-1963/64 (Dar Es Salaam: Government Printer, 1962), p. 49.

36. Five-Year Plan 1964-69, Vol. I, pp. 8 and 91.

37. Three-Year Plan 1961/62-1963/64, p. 50; and Five-Year Plan 1964-69, Vol. I, p. 91.

38. See George Dalton, "Development of Subsistence and Peasant Economies in Africa," International Social Science Journal, XVI (1964), pp. 378-389; and Bert F. Hoselitz, "Social Stratification and Economic Development," International Social Science Journal, XVI (1964), pp. 237-251.

39. See Local Government Memoranda, Part 1, No. 1 (Dar Es Salaam: Government Printer, 1954), p. 3; and East Africa, Royal Commission, 1953-55 Report (London: HMSO, 1955), p. 14.

40. Britain ruled Tanganyika from 1917 to 1961, first as a mandate under the League of Nations and then as a trusteeship under the United Nations.

41. See J. P. Moffett (ed.), Handbook of Tanganyika (Dar Es Salaam: Government Printer, 1958), p. 101; "Dispatch from Governor, Tanganyika, No. 88," September 10, 1950 (London: HMSO, 1951), pp. 4-6; S. N. Varma et al., Tanganyika, A Background Study (New Delhi, India: African Publications, 1961), p. 24; and Charlotte Leubuscher, Tanganyika Territory (London: Oxford University Press, 1944), pp. 6-21.

42. Sir Donald Cameron, "Principles of Native Administration and Their Application, 1930," Government Memoranda, No. 1, Part 1, p. 2.

43. Moffett, Handbook, p. 100; and Government Memoranda, No. 1, Part 1, pp. 1-2.

44. Varma, Tanganyika, p. 24. For a discussion of tribal loyalty, see William Watson, Tribal Cohesion in a Money Economy (Manchester: Manchester University Press, 1958).

45. Tanganyika Under United Kingdom Administration: 1954, p. 15; Tanganyika Under United Kingdom Administration: 1960, p. 20; Government Memoranda, No. 1, Part 1, p. 10; and A. W. Kent, Report on the Services to be Administered by Local Authorities in Tanganyika and the Consequential Financial Arrangements (Dar Es Salaam: Government Printer, 1962).

46. Tanganyika Under United Kingdom Administration: 1958 and 1959, p. 68. See also S. Rowland Simpson, "Land Tenure: Some Explanations and Definitions," Journal of African Administration, VI (April, 1954), pp. 50-64.

47. E. B. Dobson, "Comparative Land Tenure of Ten Tanganyika Tribes," Journal of African Administration, VI (April, 1954), p. 82.

48. See EARC, 1953-55 Report, p. 284; IBRD, pp. 77-78; and Pierre De Schlippe, Shifting Cultivation in Africa (London: Routledge and Kegan Paul, 1956).

49. Colin Clark and Margaret Haswell note that there is a high initial labor effort to the clearing of land, but that over-all the amount of effort involved in shifting cultivation is less than that used in sedentary agriculture. Colin Clark and Margaret Haswell, The Economics of Subsistence Agriculture (London: Macmillan and Company, 1964), p. 33.

50. See Eileen Jensen Krige, "Economics of Exchange in a Primitive Society," The South African Journal of Economics, IX (1941), pp. 1-21; and George M. Foster, "Peasant Society and the Image of Limited Goods," American Anthropologist, 67 (April, 1965), pp. 293-315.

51. EARC, 1953-55 Report, p. 185.

52. P. H. Gulliver, "The Evolution of Arusha Trade, " Markets in Africa, ed. , Paul Bohannan and George Dalton (Chicago: Northwestern University Press, 1962), p. 248.

53. EARC, 1953-55 Report, p. 287. See also Montague Yudelman, Africans on the Land (Cambridge: Harvard University Press, 1964), p. 99.

54. Dobson, "Land Tenure, " p. 82.

55. See ibid. , pp. 80-91; Simpson, "Land Tenure: Some Explanations and Definitions, " pp. 50-64; and John Middleton, "Trade and Markets Among the Lugbara of Uganda, " Markets in Africa, pp. 561-578.

56. EARC, 1953-55 Report, p. 287; and IBRD, pp. 84-86.

57. IBRD, pp. 116-117.

58. See EARC, 1953-55 Report, pp. 290-293; IBRD, p. 105; and Yudelman, Africans on the Land, p. 207 for a similar view.

59. Yudelman, Africans on the Land, pp. 207-213; and Theodore W. Schultz, Transforming Traditional Agriculture (New Haven: Yale University Press, 1964).

60. IBRD, p. 105.

61. Ibid.; George Dalton, "Traditional Production in Primitive African Economies, " Quarterly Journal of Economics, LXXVI, pp. 360-378; Yudelman, Africans on the Land, pp. 94-99; and Hoselitz, "Social Stratification and Economic Development, " pp. 237-251.

62. See W. O. Jones, "Economic Man in Africa, " Food Research Institute Studies, I (May, 1960), pp. 107-134; S. D. Neumark, "Economic Development and Economic Incentives, " The South African Journal of Economics, XXVI (1958), pp. 55-63; P. H. Gulliver, Labour Migration in a Rural Society (Kampala, Uganda: East African Institute of Social Research, 1955); and Harold Schneider, "Economics in East African Aboriginal Societies, "

Economic Transition in Africa, ed. Melville J. Herskovitts and Mitchell Harwitz (London: Routledge and Kegan Paul, 1964), pp. 53-76.

63. See Tanganyika Standard, May 14, 1964, p. 2.

64. IBRD, p. 11; EARC, 1953-55 Report, pp. 280-281; and Stahl, Sail, pp. 51-56.

65. EARC, 1953-55 Report, pp. 281-282.

66. Stahl, Sail, p. 55.

67. S. Herbert Frankel, "Concepts of Income and Welfare-- In Advanced and Developed Societies--With Special Reference to the Intercomparability of National Income Aggregates, " Income and Wealth Series III, ed. Milton Gilbert (Cambridge: Bowes and Bowes, 1953), p. 166.

68. Reverend P. O. Moss, "Cattle in Bahaya, " Anthropological Quarterly (January, 1954), pp. 23-29.

69. J. C. Carms, Bush and Boma (London: J. Murray, 1959), p. 32.

70. EARC, 1953-55 Report, p. 282.

71. Five-Year Plan 1964-69, Vol. I, pp. 26-27; and Stahl, Sail, p. 56.

72. Five-Year Plan 1964-69, Vol. I, pp. 26-27.

73. E. H. Winter, "Livestock Markets Among the Iraqw of Northern Tanganyika, " Markets in Africa, pp. 465-468.

74. Ibid. , p. 465.

75. Five-Year Plan 1964-69, Vol. II, p. 12.

76. Tanganyika, "Memoranda No. 15 to the Rural Settlement Commission" (Dar Es Salaam: Treasury, 1963), unpublished.

77. Five-Year Plan 1964-69, Vol. I, p. 33; and "Memoranda No. 15."

78. Five-Year Plan 1964-69, Vol. I, pp. 33-34.

79. This is the difference between the 150 shillings paid by the estate and the 30 shillings government subsidy.

NOTES TO CHAPTER 5

1. Tanganyika, Statistical Abstract: 1963 (Dar Es Salaam: Government Printer, 1963); and The Republic of Tanganyika, Annual Report of the Ministry for Communications, Power and Works, 1962 (Dar Es Salaam: Government Printer, 1964).

2. J. P. Moffett (ed.), Handbook of Tanganyika (Dar Es Salaam: Government Printer, 1958), p. 81; and Tanganyika, Statistical Abstract: 1963.

3. The United Republic of Tanganyika and Zanzibar, Five-Year Plan for Economic and Social Development, 1st July, 1964-30th June, 1969, Vol. I (Dar Es Salaam: Government Printer, 1964), p. 57.

4. This is also the opinion of the IBRD mission. International Bank for Reconstruction and Development, The Economic Development of Tanganyika (Baltimore: Johns Hopkins Press, 1961), p. 247.

5. Tanganyika, Development Plan for Tanganyika 1961/62-1963/64 (Dar Es Salaam: Government Printer, 1962), p. 29; and IBRD, p. 273.

6. IBRD, p. 277.

7. Three-Year Plan 1961/62-1963/64, p. 14.

8. Five-Year Plan 1964-69, Vol. I, pp. 54-55.

9. IBRD, p. 243; and East Africa, Royal Commission, 1953-55 Report (London: HMSO, 1955), p. 204.

10. See J. E. Goldthorpe, "An African Elite," British
     Journal of Sociology, VI (March, 1955), pp. 31-47; and
     Walter Elkan, "A Half Century of Cotton Marketing in
     Uganda," Indian Journal of Economics, XXXVIII (April,
     1958), pp. 365-374.

11. Moffett, Handbook, p. 300; and The Economist Intelligence
     Unit, A Survey of Wholesale and Retail Trade in Tangan-
     yika (London: The Economist Intelligence Unit Limited,
     December, 1962), p. 20.

12. African Recorder, September 10-23, 1963, p. 517.

13. Tanganyika Standard, May 1, 1964, p. 3.

14. Moffett, Handbook, p. 300.

15. Fergus Chalmers Wright, African Consumers (Colonial
     Research Studies, No. 17; London: HMSO, 1955), p. 11.
     For a similar view, see B. M. Niculescu, "Trade in
     Africa," Kyklos, VIII, Fasc. 4 (1955), pp. 422-426.

16. Wright, African Consumers, p. 39.

17. A Survey of Wholesale and Retail Trade, pp. 38-39.

18. Ibid., pp. 38-40.

19. EARC, 1953-55 Report, p. 202; and Wright, African
     Consumers, pp. 52-53; Goldthorpe, "An African Elite,"
     pp. 31-47.

20. Wright, African Consumers, pp. 51-52.

21. Ibid., pp. 40-41; and H. C. G. Hawkins, Wholesale and
     Retail Trade in Tanganyika (New York: Frederick A.
     Praeger, 1965), pp. 32-54.

22. Edwin R. Dean, "Social Determinants of Price in Several
     African Markets," Economic Development and Cultural
     Change, XI (April, 1963), pp. 239-256.

23. Hawkins, Wholesale and Retail Trade, p. 151.

24. Ibid.

25. Wright, African Consumers, pp. 50-60.

26. See "Seminar Report, Problems of Socialist Transforma-
    tion in Developing Countries" (Indian Council for Africa
    at Delhi University, January 18-19, 1964), Africa
    Quarterly, A Journal of African Affairs, IV (April-June,
    1964), pp. 30-47; Vincent Grogan, "Problems of the New
    African States," Studies, An Irish Quarterly Review, LI
    (1962), p. 144; and Julius Nyerere, Speech at Opening of
    Parliament, December 10, 1962.

27. Five-Year Plan 1964-69, Vol. I , p. 42.

28. See Chapter 211, "Cooperative Societies," The Laws of the
    Tanganyika Territory, Prepared Under the Authority of
    the Laws Ordinance, 1947, by Sir Donald Kingdom (London:
    Wartmoughs LTD. , 1947), pp. 2662-2687.

29. Ibid. , and T. R. Sadlier, The Cooperative Movement in
    Tanganyika (Dar Es Salaam: Tanganyika Standard Ltd.),
    p. 8.

30. Five-Year Plan 1964-69, Vol. I, p. 41.

31. IBRD, p. 124.

32. Sadlier, The Cooperative Movement, p. 3.

33. Chapter 211, "Cooperative Societies," Section 4, p. 2663.

34. Sadlier, The Cooperative Movement, pp. 12-16.

35. Tanganyika Standard, February 11, 1964, p. 4.

36. Sadlier, The Cooperative Movement, p. 19.

37. Five-Year Plan 1964-69, Vol. I, p. 42.

38. Ibid., pp. 42-43.

39. Chapter 211, "Cooperative Societies," pp. 2662-2687.

40. Ibid., Section 4 (1), p. 2676.

41. Five-Year Plan 1964-69, Vol. I, p. 41.

42. Sadlier, The Cooperative Movement, p. 16.

43. Ibid.; Tanganyika Sisal Growers Association, Annual Report 1961-62 (Dar Es Salaam: Tanganyika Standard Ltd., 1962); and TSGA, Annual Report 1964-65.

44. Chapter 284, Supplement 57, "African Agricultural Products (Control and Marketing) Ordinance 57, " July 15, 1949, as Revised 1951, 1952, 1954 and 1958 (Dar Es Salaam: Government Printer, 1958), Section 3 (1), p. 281.

45. Ibid., Section 8, p. 4.

46. Ibid., Subsidiary, G.N. No. 94 of 1952.

47. Tanganyika, Annual Report on Cooperative Development 1960 (Dar Es Salaam: Government Printer, 1963), p. 17; and Tanganyika, The Cotton Industry--Questions and Answers (Dar Es Salaam: Government Printer, 1954), p. 2.

48. Chapter 284, Supplement 57, "African Agricultural Products, " Section 7.

49. Ibid., Section 2.

50. IBRD, p. 126. See also EARC, 1953-55 Report, p. 287.

51. See Tanganyika, Annual Report on Cooperative Development 1960; and Chapter 284, "The Nyamerembe Native Tobacco (Levy) Order, " G.N. 1958.

52. Chapter 284, "African Agricultural Products, " Section 14 (1).

53. This type of scheme has been used in other African countries for the same purpose. See P. T. Bauer, "Issues in Commodity Stabilization in Africa, " Economic Development for Africa South of the Sahara, ed. E. A. G.

Robinson (London: Macmillan and Company, 1964), pp.
532-553; Gerald Helleiner, "The Fiscal Role of the
Marketing Boards in Nigerian Economic Development,
1947-1961, " Economic Journal (September, 1964), pp.
582-605; and Elkan, "Cotton Marketing in Uganda. "

54. Tanganyika Standard, July 15, 1966, p. 8.

55. Bauer, "Issues in Commodity Stabilization, " p. 547.

56. IBRD, pp. 15-26; and EARC, 1953-55 Report, pp. 46-53.

57. See, for a discussion of the spread of new ideas through
the introduction of a market, Paul Bohannan, "The Impact
of Money on an African Subsistence Economy, " The
Journal of Economic History, XIX (December, 1959);
and Montague Yudelman, Africans on the Land (Cambridge:
Harvard University Press, 1964), pp. 95-99.

58. See EARC, 1953-55 Report, pp. 46-53.

59. Tanganyika Standard, May 13, 1964, p. 3.

60. EARC, 1953-55 Report, p. 68.

61. John Bellamy, The Cotton Industry of Tanganyika (Dar Es
Salaam: Lint and Seed Marketing Board, n. d.).

62. Tanganyika, Annual Report on Cooperative Development
1960, p. 18.

63. Tanganyika Standard, March 26, 1964, p. 1.

64. Chapter 211, "Cooperative Societies, " Section 38 (4).

65. The statistical agency of Tanganyika treats the per unit
taxes on agricultural output as profit taxes. See Tanganyika, Gross Domestic Product of Tanganyika 1954-57
(Dar Es Salaam: Government Printer, 1959), p. 2.

66. P. H. Gulliver notes that the Nyakusa have refused to
produce tobacco, because the production of subsistence
crops plus migration to wage employment is more attractive. P.H. Gulliver, Labour Migration in a Rural Society

(Kampala, Uganda: East African Institute of Social
Research, 1955).

67. Tanganyika Standard, July 15, 1966, pp. 4, 7, and 8.

NOTES TO CHAPTER 6

1. International Bank for Reconstruction and Development,
    The Economic Development of Tanganyika (Baltimore:
    Johns Hopkins Press, 1961), p. 249.

2. IBRD, pp. 249-250; Tanganyika, Development Plan for
    Tanganyika 1961/62-1963/64 (Dar Es Salaam: Govern-
    ment Printer, 1962), pp. 47-48; and The United Republic
    of Tanganyika and Zanzibar, Five-Year Plan for Economic
    and Social Development, 1st July, 1964-30th June, 1969,
    Vol. I (Dar Es Salaam: Government Printer, 1964), pp.
    51-55.

3. See IBRD, p. 249; Three-Year Plan 1961/62-1963/64,
    pp. 47-48; and Five-Year Plan 1964-69, Vol. I, pp. 51-55.

4. Tanganyika, Statistical Abstract: 1962 (Dar Es Salaam:
    Government Printer, 1962); and Tanganyika, Statistical
    Abstract: 1963.

5. Tanganyika, Statistical Abstract: 1963.

6. East Africa, Royal Commission, 1953-55 Report (London:
    HMSO, 1955), p. 146.

7. Tanganyika, Statistical Abstract: 1962 and 1963.

8. Kathleen M. Stahl, Tanganyika, Sail in the Wilderness
    (Netherlands: Moulton and Company, 1961), p. 72.

9. J. E. Goldthorpe, Outlines of East African Society
    (Kampala, Uganda: Makerere College, 1959), p. 152.

10. Arthur D. Little, Tanganyika Industrial Development
    (Dar Es Salaam: Government Printer, 1961), p. 27.

11. EARC, 1953-55 Report, p. 148.

12. Ibid.

13. See EARC, 1953-55 Report, p. 153; P. H. Gulliver,
    Labour Migration in a Rural Society (Kampala, Uganda:
    East African Institute of Social Research, 1955); I.
    Schapera, Migrant Labour and Tribal Life (London:
    Oxford University Press, 1947); Goldthorpe, Outlines
    of East African Society, p. 151; and M. J. B. Molohan,
    Detribalization (Dar Es Salaam: Government Printer,
    1959), pp. 1-10.

14. There are many exceptions. If the distance from home is
    great, the African may remain away for several years,
    remitting funds to his family for the purchase of food and
    aid in agricultural work. See Gulliver, Labour Migration.

15. See Tanganyika, Report of the Territorial Minimum Wage
    Board (Dar Es Salaam: Government Printer, 1962); and
    Tanganyika, Budget Survey 1965-66, p. 26.

16. African Diary, January 12-18, 1962, p. 955.

17. Tanganyika Standard, March 13, 1964, p. 1 and March 14,
    1964, p. 1.

18. EARC, 1953-55 Report, p. 147.

19. International Labour Office, Measurement of Under-
    employment, Report prepared for the Ninth International
    Conference of Labour Statisticians (Geneva, 1957), p. 9.

20. EARC, 1953-55 Report, p. 147.

21. Tanganyika, Budget Survey 1965-66, pp. 26-28.

22. Arthur D. Little Report, p. 27.

23. This is essentially the type of unionism recommended for
    underdeveloped countries by Clark Kerr and Abraham
    Seigel, "The Structure of the Labor Force: New Dimen-
    sions and New Questions," The Industrial and Labor
    Relations Review, VIII (1955), pp. 151-168.

24. Tanganyika Standard, May 15, 1964, p. 3.

25. Government Paper No. 1, 1964, "The Establishment of Workers' Committees and Concilliation Boards" (Dar Es Salaam: Government Printer, 1964), p. 1.

26. The Trade Unions Ordinance Act, No. 51 of 1962 and the Trade Disputes (Settlement Act) 1962.

27. Tanganyika Standard, February 22, 1964, p. 1.

28. African Diary, October 19-25, 1963, p. 1403.

29. Tanganyika Standard, February 22, 1963, p. 1403.

30. Ibid.

31. African Diary, January 15-21, 1964, p. 1572.

32. Tanganyika Standard, March 2, 1964, p. 3.

33. Ibid., May 2, 1964, p. 3; and Government Paper No. 1-1964, p. 1.

34. Tanganyika Standard, February 22, 1964, p. 3.

35. Ibid., May 27, 1964, p. 5.

36. Arthur D. Little Report, p. 18.

37. Ibid., p. 27.

38. Ibid.

39. See United Kingdom, East Africa, Report of the Economic and Fiscal Commission, CMD 1279 (London: HMSO, 1961).

40. IBRD, pp. 233-234.

41. Tanganyika, Budget Survey 1965-66, pp. 18-20.

42. IBRD, p. 234. See also Arthur D. Little Report, p. 18; and Great Britain, Tanganyika Under United Kingdom Administration: 1960 (London: HMSO, 1960), p. 75.

43. Arthur D. Little Report, pp. 19-21.

44. Tanganyika, Statistical Abstract: 1962, Table L. 1, pp.
    84-86. In 1962, over 43,000 of about 85,000 people
    were engaged in this activity, or over 50 per cent.
    Tanganyika, Statistical Abstract: 1963, Table L. 1, pp.
    85-87.

45. United Republic of Tanganyika and Zanzibar, Central
    Statistical Bureau, Census of Industrial Production in
    Tanganyika 1961 (Dar Es Salaam: Government Printer,
    1964), p. 17.

46. Tanganyika, Statistical Abstract: 1963, Table L. 1, p. 87.

47. Five-Year Plan 1964-69, Vol. I, pp. 38-40.

48. Republic of Tanganyika, Ministry for Commerce and
    Industry, Annual Report of the Commerce and Industry
    Division 1963 (Dar Es Salaam: Government Printer,
    1964), p. 8.

49. African Diary, July 13-19, 1964, pp. 1339-1340.

50. Tanganyika, Annual Report of Commerce and Industry
    1963, p. 5.

51. Tanganyika Standard, July 15, 1966, p. 7.

52. For a discussion of this fund and changes in organization,
    see IBRD, pp. 117-120; and Five-Year Plan 1964-69,
    Vol. I, pp. 43-44.

53. Records of National Development Corporation.

54. The New York Times, March 30, 1964, p. 28.

55. African Recorder, January 15-18, 1962, pp. 73-74.

56. African Diary, June 22-28, 1963, p. 1213.

57. Tanganyika, Ministry for Industry and Commerce,
    Commerce and Industry in Tanganyika (Dar Es Salaam:
    The Ministry for Industry and Commerce, 1961), p. 15.

58. B. M. Niculescu, "Trade in Africa," <u>Kyklos</u>, VIII, Fasc. 4 (1955), p. 424.

59. Tanganyika Development Finance Company, Ltd., <u>TDFL</u> (Arusha: National Printers, LTD.), p. 1.

60. Tanganyika, <u>Annual Report of Commerce and Industry 1963</u>, p. 1; and <u>African Diary</u>, July 13-19, 1963, p. 1340.

61. <u>Tanganyika Standard</u>, June 15, 1964, p. 4.

62. <u>TDFL</u>, p. 1.

63. <u>Ibid.</u>, p. 3.

64. <u>The Tanganyika</u>, July 14, 1966.

NOTES TO CHAPTER 7

1. East Africa, Royal Commission, <u>1953-55 Report</u> (London: HMSO, 1955), p. 93.

2. For a similar view see <u>ibid.</u>, p. 92.

3. Tanganyika, <u>Statistical Abstract: 1963</u> (Dar Es Salaam: Government Printer, 1963), p. 111.

4. <u>Ibid.</u>, p. 106.

5. <u>Ibid.</u>

6. <u>Tanganyika Standard</u>, February 11, 1964, p. 3.

7. <u>African Recorder</u>, July 2-15, 1962, p. 216.

8. Tanganyika, <u>East Africa, The Present Monetary System and Its Future,</u> Report to the Government (Dar Es Salaam: Government Printer, 1963), p. 21.

9. <u>The Standard</u>, June 16, 1966, pp. 6-9.

10. Tanganyika, <u>Statistical Abstract: 1963</u>, p. 97.

11. The Standard, June 16, 1966, pp. 6-9.

12. Tanganyika, Development Plan for Tanganyika 1961/62-1963/64 (Dar Es Salaam: Government Printer, 1962), p. 9.

13. The United Republic of Tanganyika and Zanzibar, Five-Year Plan for Economic and Social Development, 1st July, 1964-30th June, 1969, Vol. I (Dar Es Salaam: Government Printer, 1964), p. 97.

14. Three-Year Plan 1961/62-1963/64, p. 9; and Five-Year Plan 1964-69, Vol. I, p. 97.

15. Tanganyika, Budget Survey 1965-66, pp. 35-36.

16. Tanganyika Standard, May 25, 1964, p. 2.

17. Tanganyika, Budget Survey 1965-66, p. 34.

18. Tanganyika Standard, May 26, 1964, p. 1.

19. Red China has pledged to Tanganyika a loan of ₤698,000. Tanganyika, Budget Survey 1965-66, p. 36. For Karume's remarks see Tanganyika Standard, May 26, 1964, p. 1.

ABOUT THE AUTHOR

Gilbert Rutman is Assistant Professor of Economics at West Virginia University. He received a doctorate in economics in 1965 from Duke University and also studied at Boston University. Prior to his affiliation with West Virginia Dr. Rutman taught at the University of Arizona. He has served in the Air Force, has traveled in East Africa and South Africa, and has contributed to the South African Journal of Economics and the Journal of Marketing.